PURSE
MASTERPIECES

IDENTIFICATION & VALUE GUIDE

LYNELL SCHWARTZ

COLLECTOR BOOKS
A Division of Schroeder Publishing Co., Inc.

Front cover, background: Raphael's *Madonna Della Sedia* glass beaded purse, very rare.

First row, left: "The New Piccadilly" enameled mesh vanity bag, very rare; trinity plate needlepoint fruit motif dance purse, $495.00 – 595.00; art nouveau glass beaded Geisha purse; $800.00 – 1,200.00, Austrian petit point figural purse, $950.00 – 1,200.00.

Second row, left: tambour worked trinity plate dance purse, $450.00 – 650.00; jewel encrusted compact purse, $650.00 – 850.00; castle scenic glass beaded purse, $2,000.00; mandalian mesh purse, rare.

Bottom: Scenic petit point purse, $495.00 – 650.00.

Back cover, background: Raphael's *Madonna Della Sedia* glass beaded purse, very rare. Left: glass beaded figural purse, very rare; barefoot angel with harp, glass beaded figural purse, rare; art nouveau jeweled moth motif mesh purse, very rare.

Cover design by Beth Summers
Book design by Heather Warren

COLLECTOR BOOKS
P.O. Box 3009
Paducah, Kentucky 42002-3009

www.collectorbooks.com

Copyright © 2004 Lynell Schwartz

The current values in this book should be used only as a guide. They are not intended to set prices, which vary from one section of the country to another. Auction prices as well as dealer prices vary greatly and are affected by condition as well as demand. Neither the author nor the publisher assumes responsibility for any losses that might be incurred as a result of consulting this guide.

Searching For A Publisher?

We are always looking for people knowledgeable within their fields. If you feel that there is a real need for a book on your collectible subject and have a large comprehensive collection, contact Collector Books.

Contents

Dedication
To Bill

Acknowledgments

A special thanks to Tara Lewis for proofreading and editing, also, Paula Higgins and Suzanne Volkner Jones. A special thanks to Dorita Hoff for her art research. Elizabeth Weyburn and Christine Bock, textile curators at the Atlanta History Museum should also be acknowledged. A thank you to Marion Held and Carmen Frisby for insights into past German culture; William Schwartz for artwork; Eric Kitik for computer expertise; and Walter Kitik for his assistance.

Introduction

The secrets behind purse development seemed to be restricted to those who long ago aspired to string the beads, knit the silk, or stitch the canvases. Details of artistic motivation were frequently confined within tautly knitted silk threads and anchored with cool glass beads. Through the years, this painstaking purse-making process has nearly become a lost and mysterious art. Until now.

The innovators responsible for their conception, through the expert use of color and technique, have long since passed. However, their unique visions, derived from an array of artistic genres (including stories from Scripture, architectural marvels, antiquated theatrics, significant literary works, master paintings, and important historical portraits), remain in the intricate patterns and meticulous details of these fashion accoutrements. With these profound subjects providing inspiration, these artists devised patterns and initiated handmade production of masterpiece purses.

Like classic paintings, purses silently convey fascinating stories. The bags, themselves, offer clues to help divulge these narratives today. How a purse is made may tell us who made it. Proper identification of materials can suggest where the bag originated. And, as with all antiques, careful evaluation of materials can be instrumental in dating the piece.

Subject matter, too, speaks volumes. Years after these bags ceased to be knitted or sewn, these prudently chosen themes can provide insight into the past, indicating why these purses were made. With information gleaned from many sources, they acquired a renewed voice and the mystery surrounding these vintage purses is finally resolved.

Through collecting, researching, and writing about vintage purses for over a decade, the lesson learned has been to treasure them as one would fine art. Just as art generally rises in value, so have fabulous purses, and like their counterparts, we are fortunate that they can be enjoyed for their beauty while they appreciate in value.

Recognizing Purses as Art

Imagine a beautiful painted scene with its intricate detail and multitude of shades by Raphael or Fragonard. Now try to envision one of these famous oil paintings or dreamy watercolors miraculously transformed into tiny glass beads and hand carried in the form of a purse. As impossible as this may seem, it was actually done, and accomplished with such artistic style that these special purses have forged a category of their own: purse masterpieces.

Never before has the intimate link between fine art and the fashion history of purses been examined. Hand strung with care and containing thousands of fine glass beads or dexterously sewn with tiny silk stitches, these well-thought-out scenes, figures, flowers, and abstracts were remarkable achievements. These purses, like their magnificent counterparts, have become collectible works of art in their own right.

Purses re-creating famous paintings have depicted masterpieces like that of Raphael's *Madonna della Sedia*, or an important religious painting such as Millet's *The Angelus*, or his controversial work, *The Gleaners*.

An unfinished glass beaded purse captures the Tondo style artwork of Raphael's Madonna della Sedia (1513 – 14) which expertly uses soft curves fitted into a rounded shape. 9½ x 8. From the collection of Marion Held. Very rare.

Prior to photography, it was the paintings, watercolors, drawings, and other visuals that were more than mere portrayals of events — they were methods of communication. Elaborate purses reminiscent of great art are like windows, offering a special glimpse into these fascinating earlier times through the unique interpretation of the bead worker. The purse creator adds individuality to the original artist's subject matter by virtue of its extraordinary composition and creative choices decided upon during the making of each bag.

In addition to subjects taken from beautiful illustrated art, ideas were also borrowed from theatrical and literary art. Subject matter including the Comedia de l'arte, featuring Harlequin; adventure novels, with scenes from *Robinson Crusoe*; or fairytale characters such as *Sleeping Beauty*, were lavishly copied in colored beads or painstakingly stitched to the purse. In fact, arguably the greatest piece of literature ever written, The Bible had scripture transformed into glass beads depicting Jesus and the Samaritan woman.

Some tapestry and petit point subjects were created in styles like the French Boucher's romantic pastoral scenes. And certain beaded purse themes resemble figures from Russian-born Erte's art deco style fashion drawings.

Egyptian motifs in glass beads are another way the purse is made to resemble an earlier art form. Consider the extraordinary detail of a throne found in the tomb of Tutankhamun expertly reproduced in tiny glass beads as a purse.

Hand-painted miniatures popular during Edwardian and Victorian times are accomplished on purse lids depicting famous early landmarks in France. They, too, may be considered works of art re-emerging in the form of purses.

The likeness of a famous person, such as the Baron de Saint-Julien's mistress as she merrily kicks off a slipper, is depicted in Fragonard's painting, *The Swing*. Madame de Pompadour's painted image was generously commissioned numerous times during the reign of King Louis XV. Aside from being universally recognized portraits on canvas, the works were later re-created as functional works of art—purses!

Although vintage purses were made in strikingly close resemblance to significant paintings, this is not to suggest a purse must have duplicated a known masterpiece to be a painstaking representation of artistry in its own right. For instance, a glass beaded purse made in the likeness of a glorious angel holding a musical instrument is truly a work of art. A tiny stitched petit point with a heavy silver frame featuring the likeness of St. George on horseback is considered a shining example of silversmith's expertise.

Additionally, illustrated purses and frames are also taken into account, as evidenced by the original design art from The EA Bliss Company which eventually became the property of The Napier Company in Meriden, Connecticut. These outstanding sketches, often tipped in color on special wax paper, were exceptional and unique designs created with the intent for production.

In 1924, Emma Post Barbour recognized the beauty and artistry of the beaded purse with these prophetic words: "...and a work of art always lives, becoming enhanced by age in both value and sentiment."

This brings us to a most intriguing example of artwork in the form of an unfinished purse. The lovely piece captures the work of Raphael (Raffaello Sanzio) in his painting called *Madonna della Sedia* (1513 – 14). This painting was beautifully interpreted in the beadworker's hands.

Madonna della Sedia translates to Madonna of the Chair. The style of the painting is known as Tondo, the Italian term for circular in which the artist expertly uses soft curves fitted into a rounded shape, a procedure clearly depicted on the unfinished purse. The soft curves encourage the vision of an intimate family assembly. Everything in the scene is aimed at harmonious balance as each figure exists as an essential part. It is a striking example of Raphael's significant contribution to the paintings of High Renaissance.

Raphael was born in Urbino in 1483. His father, Giovanni Santi, considered a minor artist, gave Raphael his first instruction in the techniques of painting. He sent Raphael to Perugia, to become an apprentice under the highly regarded artist, Perugino. From this teacher, Raphael learned to avoid excessive detail in his work as shown in *Madonna della Sedia*. He remained faithful to the Perugino school in his earlier works and this privileged education helped him to express the spirit of the High Renaissance. Raphael was such a talented student that it is difficult to distinguish between Perugino's and Raphael's earlier works.

In 1504, at the age of 21, Raphael went to Florence. At this time Leonardo da Vinci had just returned from Milan and the public was marveling at his *Mona Lisa*, Fra Bartolommeo was exhibiting his *Last Judgement*, and Michelangelo had completed his *David*.

Some artists represented people and things not as they really were, but according to socially acceptable standards of beauty, known as the "principle of idealization." This is fulfilled not only in *Madonna della Sedia*, through the calm contemplative expressions, dainty mouths, and the serene beauty of the woman holding the child, but also clearly translated through the use of beads. The approach was learned from his teacher.

As time went on, he learned to modify the technique and assimilate the styles of da Vinci and Michelangelo. Michelangelo's influence on Raphael's painting can be seen more distinctly when the figures in Raphael's pictures acquired more voluptuous bodies following the unveiling of the Sistine Chapel ceiling in 1509. Great masters were motivated and influenced by each other's work. Several artists emulated the graceful head of Raphael's Virgin for their own. While Raphael had painted many enchanting variations on the theme of the Virgin and Child, he also had the skill to depict nearly every kind of figure, from a modest young mother to an apprehensive old man.

The subject of this purse was the most popular and beautiful of his Madonnas. Raphael's Madonnas were feminine and graceful, and copies of *Madonna della Sedia* adorned all the Paris studios at the time.

Sadly, Raphael died young, in 1520 at the age of 37 years old. In 1541, long after Raphael's death, it is surprising to find a tinge of jealousy in Michalengelo's letter about him, complaining that "everything he knew about art he got from me." Today, Raphael is often remembered as a painter of the Madonnas.

Another fascinating example of a purse being re-created from an earlier art form is the marvelous glass-beaded purse of a couple bowed in prayer during the noon devotional. The subject of this purse is

This fine glass-beaded figural purse is based on the painting, *The Angelus* (1859) by Jean-Francois Millet, of a couple bowed in prayer during the noon devotional. French painter Millet, born to peasants, fancied works with soft muted colors marked by a genuine respect for rural laborers. 8 x 11. From the collection of Joyce Morgan, photograph by Harry Barth. Rare.

based on the painting called *The Angelus* (1859), made by Jean-Francois Millet (1814 – 1875) that hangs in the Louvre. *The Angelus* depicts a Roman Catholic devotional prayer recited at morning, noon, and night to commemorate the Annunciation, the angel Gabriel's announcement of the Incarnation.

The setting of *The Angelus*, captured beautifully on the purse, is a potato field where a pair of workers have been bagging potatoes. The season would have been late summer or early fall. Potatoes recently dug, their withered vines scattering the ground, fill sacks placed in the wheelbarrow to the right of the woman.

An example of this purse exists in fine glass beads, with another version in cut steel beads. The one with steel beads is large and well executed. The beads are more vivid than expected, yet astonishingly, still in keeping with Millet's vision of muted colors.

Insight to the French painter's use of colors and his choice of subjects becomes evident with details of his upbringing. As a peasant raised on a farm, he demonstrated artistic ability early in life. His early studies were with the Cherbourg painter Langlois de Chevreville. He was then sent to Paris in 1837, spending two difficult years in the studio of the demanding Paul Delaroche, who, surprisingly, considered him unteachable.

Like many young artists who struggle, such was the early fate of Millet, when instead of painting from his heart, painted on demand. To earn a living, during these difficult times, Millet made pastels in imitation of rococo masters, as well as portraits and commercial signs. He exhibited his first portrait at the Salon in 1840. In 1841, he revisited Cherbourg and married Pauline Ono, with whom he returned to Paris in 1842. She died in 1844, the same year he again exhibited at the Salon with *The Milkmaid* and *The Riding Lesson*. He remarried in 1845 and held a successful exhibition in Le Havre.

In the late 1840s, after early attempts at religious and classical subjects, Millet found his characteristic

French cut steel beaded figural purse depicting Millet's *The Angelus*, of a Roman Catholic devotional prayer recited morning, noon, and night to commemorate the Annunciation. On the label, sewn onto the lining: "La Raison Made in France." 8½ x 11½. From the collection of Kirsten Recce. Rare.

theme in his romanticized depictions of peasant life. The suppressed messages he previously wished to express to the world now brilliantly came forth from his brush. Millet's work, including *The Angelus*, was marked by a deeply rooted respect for the rural laborers with whom he remained in close contact. His reapers, gleaners, and woodcutters are portrayed with a quiet, often immense, dignity. His method combining somber colors along with simple groupings of noble peasants at work were to strongly influence future artists.

Reproductions of *The Angelus* have hung in many classrooms and Sunday schools. The humble background of the artist may shed some light on the reason for the predominantly earthy tones of the painting, transformed beautifully into a glass and metal beaded purse. The soft, natural colors and balance of the artwork are metamorphosed through beads.

One of Millet's hundreds of works is *Les Glaneuses*, or *The Gleaners*, beautifully depicted on a steel beaded, jewel framed purse. "Glean" means to gather grain or other produce left by reapers. Capturing peasants in the midst of their routine chores, it is the artist's best known work. Poor gleaners depicted here were intending to make good use of the residuals left after the harvest. This needy act helped portray the peasants in a favorable light, quite literally as well as figuratively.

The painting shows three gleaning women bathed in a golden light that appears to add a quiet dignity. Through the inspired use of soft color, Millet blended the figures to a tone almost equal to that of the earth itself, implying that the peasants were one with the earth. None of these subtle, but intentional, color tones were lost in the transition to purse form.

The women purposely have no faces, possibly resembling "the three fates of pauperism," or perhaps, that they could represent the fate of anyone. Undoubtedly, this painting is more than a depiction of peasant life. It is a social critique, documenting the struggle of the peasant

---

(Top) The subject of this jewel framed steel beaded purse is taken from Millet's painting, *The Gleaners*, showing three women bathed in a golden light gathering grain left by reapers. It became a national inspiration and is still one of France's most cherished works. 8 x 11. From the collection of Paula Jay Wolslager. Rare.

(Bottom) Meticulous details of this large fine glass beaded purse scene include the plaid pattern on the woman's skirt and the grain of the wooden door. The figures peer into the distance at a mysterious unidentified source. The pointing finger of the infant suggests a style often occurring in Leonardo da Vinci's work, a gesture that evokes speculation. 9½ x 15. Author's collection. Very rare.

class, emphasizing their work to collect the few scraps left by the rich, who are only blurs in the far distance. Millet drew criticism for the scene, and it was the basis for energetic debates. Art critics of that era could not easily embrace mere peons in the martyr's role. When humble folk became the chief subjects of paintings, it accentuated the struggle between two classes and sparked much controversy.

Along with all its meaning and symbolism, Millet included one final aspect to attract the observer. Patterns of heavy shadows are meant to divert the viewer's attention from the meager bundles of the gleaning women to the abundant stacks of the havest. This technique makes the contrast between rich and poor all the more obvious.

At first disliked by some, *The Gleaners* eventually became a national inspiration to French people. They began to personify themselves as the faceless, hardworking gleaners represented in the painting, engaged in a struggle with a distant oppressor. Over the years the work has seen many revivals in popularity including its replication in beaded purse form. In WWI, it was even used on army recruitment posters in France. Today it is still one of France's most cherished works.

Following the 1848 Revolution, Millet settled in Barbizon where he was to spend his remaining years painting the rural scenes where he lived. He created many seascapes in the early 1870s when the Franco-Prussian War prompted his return to Cherbourg. During the height of his popularity, in the later nineteenth century, his work was acquired by many American museums. The Louvre possesses his most notable examples, including *The Angelus* (1859), re-created in the form a purse; *The Gleaners* (1857), also re-emerging in purse form; and *Church at Greville* (1871).

A petit point purse recalls Jean-Honoré Fragonard's most famous painting entitled *The Swing* (1766 – 1767). Commissioned by the Baron de Saint-Julien, it is he who appears in the left-hand corner of the painting while his mistress floats above on the swing. (The Baron does not appear on the purse, since every detail could not be duplicated exactly as in the original work.) The mistress, gleefully kicking off her slipper, exudes the uninhibited joy of her ride while the baron seems amused by her antics. Originally titled *Les Hasards heureux de L'escarpolette* (The Happy Hazards of The Swing), which suggests the carefree spirit of the painting, it is one of the most familiar images in eighteenth century art. It is no wonder that this scene is the focus of many lovely vintage beaded and petit point purses.

Considered the last great painter of the French rococo style, Fragonard served a four-year apprenticeship with Francois Boucher. In 1756, he went to Rome to study and found his greatest source of

This petit point purse re-creates Jean-Honoré Fragonard's most famous painting, *The Swing*. It is no wonder that this scene is the focal point of many lovely vintage purses including beaded, petit point, and others. The figure of the woman floating through the air with the appearance of weightlessness is said to be one of the great triumphs of his art. 6 x 8. From the collection of Shara Stewart. $800.00 – 1,000.00.

inspiration in the passionate works by the Italian baroque painters. On his return to Paris, Fragonard gained membership in the Academy with a large history painting, winning additional acclaim at the Salon. He did not, however, follow up this success, but turned to painting on a more intimate scale, specializing in lively erotic pictures that secured his place among Parisians.

This painting was said to have been Fragonard's best for color and brushwork. The beautiful figure of the woman effortlessly gliding through the air with near weightlessness is said to be one of the great triumphs of his art. In 1859 the Louvre had the opportunity to buy this painting but surprisingly declined.

Purse subjects were not always taken directly from famous paintings but were also copied from their influential styles. The artwork of Francois Boucher (1703 – 1770), one of the most successful French painters of his time and the favorite of Louis XV and his mistress, Madame de Pompadour portrays lovely women, swirls, colorful flowers, shining satins, and puffy taffetas while suggesting erotic elegance and elaborate femininity. He was master of the decorative rococo style, illustrating the elegance of French court life in the eighteenth century in his paintings.

The romantic tapestry scenic purse depicting a pair of lovers lounging in a pasture is strongly reminiscent of Boucher's work, specifically of a painting entitled, *Autumn*. The correlation can be made regardless of the different garb the figures wear. (This is chiefly due to the purse maker's unique interpretation of the original artwork.) She is looking downward in the painting as she does on the purse with her head tilted at virtually the same angle. She has a distinctively delicate oval-shaped face and her demure is consistent with the lady in the painting. Suggestive of the painting in purse form, although not an exact duplicate, it was executed in just the way the tapestry designer intended.

The positioning of the gentleman's is nearly identical and his attentions are entirely hers, in both purse and painting.

The mannered poses of the main figures are indicative of the artist's association with the Opera Comique and Ballet where he was a designer of exotic sets and beautiful costumes. *Autumn* is one of a series of paintings by Boucher, each depicting romantic figures in four seasonal settings.

Boucher's pastoral scenes and erotic subjects were his most popular works. Paintings of bucolic scenes became fashionable in Europe during the sixteenth and seventeenth centuries, and were largely derived from poetry. They usually focused on simple activities taking place in rustic settings. In one of Boucher's paintings, a shephardess feeds a shepherd with a grape, an action that, as the picture's title, *Are They Thinking of*

The romantic tapestry scenic purse with a pair of lovers lounging in a pasture is strongly reminiscent of the artwork of Francois Boucher (1703 – 1770). This lovely two-sided tapestry purse appears to be taken after the likeness of a painting called *Autumn*, one of a series of paintings by Boucher, each depicting romantic figures in seasonal settings. His work portrays pretty woman, swirls, and flowers while suggesting erotic elegance and elaborate femininity. Intricate 800 silver figural frame. 8 x 9. The Curiosity Shop. $750.00 – 950.00.

Grapes? (1747), suggests, has sensual undertones.

The painting is obviously not a realistic depiction of country life. The figures are elegantly dressed and beautifully groomed. Their clothes are spotlessly clean and show no traces of dirt or toil. The contented sheep lie quietly at their feet, and the landscape is deliberately idealistic. These types of scenes, with lovers, lambs, and landscapes, were often subjects for purses of many types.

This charming and sentimental vision reflects in part the attitudes of Boucher's eighteenth century French patrons towards the countryside. As prosperous town-dwellers, they probably had little idea of the toils of rural life. To them, the country offered a pleasant retreat from the pressures of living in town, and the vision of a simpler, purer life. The realty of actual farm work did not hold a place in this idealized thinking.

Ethel Matthews.

Much of the period artwork from Egypt has firmly withstood the test of time, providing us with fascinating insight to the past. Perhaps Pharaohs, whose bodies were given great preparation and ceremony in a vast attempt to defeat mortality, were able to do so, to some extent, as evidenced by artwork discoveries, purses made after them, and the unwavering gaze of the haunting mummies that have been unearthed. While no new breath of life fills their lungs, the artwork surrounding their reigns majestically lives on. This art has been lovingly re-created through the beaded artwork of vintage Egyptian motif purses.

Many purses were made depicting Egyptian figures, hieroglyphics, and pyramids during this Egyptian revival period. Some contain French celluloid frames or are of celluloid in their entirety, molded into the shapes of Pharaohs, Sphinxes, eagles, suns, and other subjects of ancient Egyptian nostalgia during this period of heightened awareness.

One example, the lovely glass beaded purse with Egyptian figures, is taken from the artwork on the back of a throne found in the tomb of

Tutankhamun in the Valley of the Kings. Tutankhamun reigned from about 1334 to 1325 BC after Egypt had become the first of significance to unify under a single king during the Eighteenth Dynasty of the New Kingdom.

Interest in Egyptian artifacts peaked in the early 1920s when Howard Carter discovered what was considered the greatest find in archaeological history: the tomb of King Tutankhamun, the young Egyptian ruler. Although approximately 33 royal tombs had been unearthed prior to the discovery of this one in November of 1922, thieves had pillaged all long before.

Among the many items found in the tomb were

Artwork on the back of a throne found in the tomb of Tutankhamun, who reigned in Egypt from about 1334 to 1325 BC, is the subject matter of this beaded purse. It is remarkable how closely the scene is resembled considering the limitations of the inhibiting size and shape of each glass bead. From the detailed hieroglyphics to the curved feet of the throne the king sits on, there was great attention paid to each element, most certainly accomplished with a passion for purses as well as a genuine interest in Egyptian revival. 8 x 12. From the collection of Diane Goldfarb. Very rare.

Unique fine beaded steel figural with a Grecian influence. The various step stages of fringe in a checked pattern enhance the Greek Key motif on the surrounding border. Applied garlands of flowers decorate the gilt frame. Marked "France." 6½ x 12¼. From the collection of Kirsten Recce. $1,200.00 – 1,500.00.

made of silver, near to the queen is a table supporting a large, unusual shaped object called a broad collar.

Rays of light come from behind the royals depicting the sun disk, Aton, which is not visible on the purse. The life-sustaining power of the Aton was concerned with all lands, providing "a Nile in the sky" (rain), a very rare occurrence in Egypt.

The casual, tender moment between King Tut and Queen Ankhesenamen, without the formality and stiffness generally portrayed of royal figures, is somewhat strange in Egyptian art. This is evidenced in part by the way that she gently rests her right hand on the King's left shoulder.

It is remarkable how closely the vintage purse scene resembles the original artwork, considering the limitations of the inhibiting size and shape of each glass bead. From the elaborate hieroglyphics to the curved feet of the throne the King sits on, one can easily see that there was great attention to detail when re-creating the scene with glass beads.

personal belongings of the king which he was expected to enjoy in the afterlife, as well as funerary items such as amulets, statuettes, and tools. These priceless objects of comfort, luxury, and religious significance were buried with the Pharaoh, reflecting the attitude toward Atonism and a naturalistic style of art. His remarkable throne was also located with him, for he was likely expected to continue his reign for eternity.

This throne, made of carved wood, is covered with sheet gold and the graceful figures of Tutankhamun and his queen. The royals are inlaid with colored glass, called faience (earthenware decorated with colorful opaque glazes) and carnelian (a reddish hard gem). Their clothes are

Exhibiting a style of artwork vaguely similar to Erte's, this fine glass beaded figural purse with a pierced work 800 silver frame demonstrates a classic artistic style. 8 x 11. Author's collection. $2,000.00 + .

Based on the Italian Comedia "de l'Arte," this extraordinary glass beaded figural purse features Columbina. Crocheted header, reticule style purse. 6 x 9. From the collection of Marion Held. Rare.

The reverse side depicts Harlequin, or Arlechinno. Notice the short looped fringe at both top and bottom, and the unusual border.

Because the sun disk of the Aton and its rays are not present on the purse, one assumes that the bead worker decided it would crowd the all-important figures. Instead, the viewer's eye is drawn to the headdresses of the royals, as well as to the elaborate garb they wear and the broad collar behind the queen, all of which is meticulously detailed in beads. Even the Pharaoh's bracelet bands and sandal tops have been given unerring attention.

Every effort was made to copy this priceless piece of Egyptian art with great precision. It is certainly elaborately detailed by any estimate, particularly when taking into account the restrictive use of beads. Most likely it was undertaken with a passion for purses as well as a genuine interest in the resurrection of the tomb of King Tutankhamun. The height of the throne is 41 inches and it is on display in the Egyptian Museum, Cairo.

Vintage scenic and figural purse subjects may not be reminiscent of breathtaking illustrated art at all, but instead, are derived from theatrical art. Based on the interaction of colorful characters in lively, improvised scenarios, the Comedia de l'arte or Comedy of Artists, was popular in the marketplaces and streets of the early Italian Renaissance. While its beginnings can be traced back to ancient Roman and Greek theater, the lively antics and ancient story telling live on today in many ways.

Talented Italian street performers wore ornate masks with comical features designed to capture the attention of the audience. Combined with their unusual costumes, acrobatic skills, clever mimes, stunts, gags, and silly pranks, they provided comic

"Zum Namensjest" or For Your Saint's Day in German.

Very unusual multi-figural Harlequin purse. Enameled frame, looped fringe. 8 x 10. Author's collection. Rare.

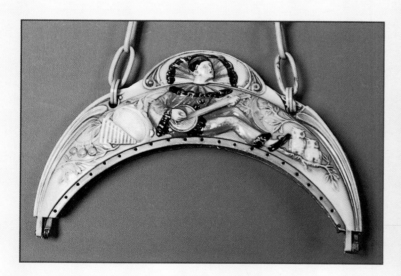

French Harlequin celluloid purse frame. Circa: 1920s. 5¾. Author's collection. $350.00 – 450.00.

The Harem "Baby"

relief from everyday worries. They performed for and were enjoyed by all social classes. Some would team up in acting troupes, making traveling stages as the popularity of this art grew in the 1500s. As language was not an issue because of practiced mimes and gestures, they were accepted wherever they traveled. Later, the tradition spread to Europe, with France adapting many of the scripted scenarios into amusing plays. From the Comedia world, popular characters such as Arlechinno (Harlequin) and Columbina emerged to reign in theatre for centuries.

The zanni, or servant type character, Harlequin, was a favorite. He was acrobatic and witty, yet childlike and passionate. He wore a cat-like mask and motley colored clothes while carrying a bat or wooden sword that appeared in many of the reproductions depicting his likeness, including the beaded purse.

Actors, writers, and artists have been inspired by the work of Comedia. Entertainers through the years have been influenced by their antics and fledgling approach to comedy. Their lively antics and ancient story telling continue on today, as pictorials — in the form of vintage purses.

Purse subject matter was also derived from famous literary adventures, like *Robinson Crusoe,* and fairy tales such as *Sleeping Beauty.*

Daniel Defoe's famous adventure novel is the story of one man's courage and ability to survive nearly independently on an uninhabited island while facing hardships and adversity in addition to the forces of nature. It recounts the tale of an English sailor marooned for twenty-seven years on a nearly deserted Caribbean island. Hunting wild boars for food, and saving his man, Friday, from a cannibal's feast, he survives the ultimate test of nature.

The glass beaded purse has two different scenes, one features a climatic rescue in which a flagship appears on the water behind Crusoe, while the ship's captain greets him on land. The

The subject matter of this purse was taken from Daniel Defoe's famous adventure novel, *Robinson Crusoe*, depicting the story of one man's courage and his ability to survive on a nearly uninhabited island while facing the forces of nature, hardships, and adversity. Fine glass beads, nineteenth century. 6½ x 8. From the collection of Marion Held. Rare.

As shown on this lovely purse, *Robinson Crusoe* recounts the tale of an English sailor marooned for twenty-seven years on a nearly deserted Caribbean island. He survives the ultimate test of nature; hunting wild boars for food and rescuing his man, Friday, from a cannibal's feast. Nineteenth century.

other depicts Friday and Crusoe in the midst of every day life on the island.

The *Sleeping Beauty* fairytale is unveiled on a colorful petit point stitched purse. The reverse side shows the strong prince nimbly making his way through the enchanted forest on his way to rescue the lovely girl. The front portrays the girl and those closest to her, stricken with sleep in the overgrown woods. Although earlier variations of the fairytale date to the 1500s, the Brothers Grimm version made it popular.

Finally, there is a purse taken from a page in what is arguably the most important piece of literature ever written: the Bible. Taken from Scripture John 4:1–42, The Woman of Samaria, a Samaritan woman and Jesus have an unexpected discussion at Jacob's well. The purse depicting this glorious colorful scene in tiny glass beads is an undeniable work of art.

Taken from Scripture John 4:1–42, The Woman of Samaria. A Samaritan woman and Jesus have an unexpected discussion at Jacob's well. Fine glass beaded purse with richly jeweled frame in blue cabochons and enamel. 6 x 7½. From the collection of Marion Held. $1,200.00+.

A rare scenic purse portraying *Sleeping Beauty* in colorful petit point stitches. The reverse side shows the prince nimbly making his way through the enchanted forest on his way to rescuing the lovely Sleeping Beauty. Although earlier variations of the fairytale date to the 1500s, the Brothers Grimm's version made it popular. 8 x 9. From the collection of Diane Goldfarb. Rare.

Nineteenth-century European silk knitted and metallic thread purse in a sectional design, typical of the period. Vandyke edging at the top, brass lid set with five hand-painted scenes under glass including Cleopatra's Needle, the Arch de Triomphe, and Nelson's Monument. 4 x 5. From the collection of Paula Higgins. $800.00 – 1,000.00.

One of many exceptional purse frame designs created at the EA Bliss Company, circa 1911. They were sketched, then tipped in color showing glorious detail, incorporating gemstones, enameling, and innovative shapes. Courtesy of the Napier Company archives.

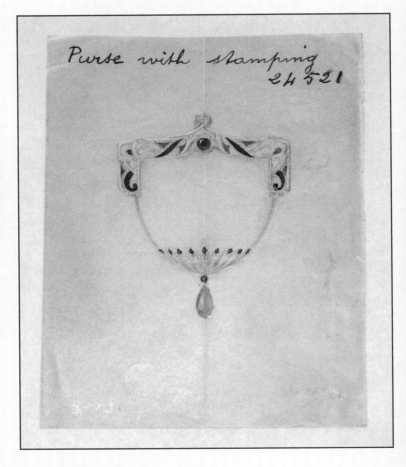

Dated 1838 on the frame's interior, this European chatelaine purse has a star bottom, tassel, and a crocheted three sectional floral motif attached to a gilt metal frame and chain, complete with finger ring. This lovely piece of artwork consists of a glass-protected scene of a lithographed print inset with people dressed in a manner indicative of the era as they leisurely stroll around a massive public building. 2½ x 9. From the collection of Paula Higgins. $750.00 – 850.00.

Although it is often referred to as "The Butterfly Hunters" or "The Butterfly Catchers," this fine glass beaded purse more accurately depicts two maidens with an oar heading toward water for a canoe or boat ride. Elaborate jeweled frame with large glass central stone. 8 x 13. Author's collection. $2,500.00+.

A maiden dances in a garden setting. Fine glass beaded purse, enameled frame. 8 x 11. Author's collection. $2500.00+.

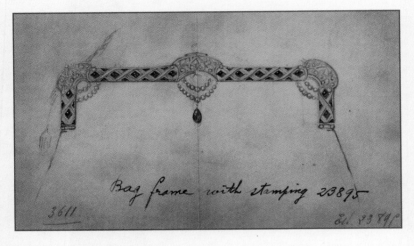

Dated February of 1912, the artwork for this unique purse frame design was created for E.A. Bliss. Courtesy of The Napier Company archives.

An exquisite tapestry purse depicting three figures with a different scene on the reverse. Elaborate jeweled frame with genuine cameo. 7 x 8. The Curiosity Shop. $800.00 – 1,000.00.

Austrian petit point with a classical scene. Bezel set stones decorate the heavy cast frame. St. George and the dragon appear on both sides of the frame, a jeweled cherub swings from the pendant drop. 7½ x 7½. From the collection of Paula Higgins. $950.00 – 1,200.00.

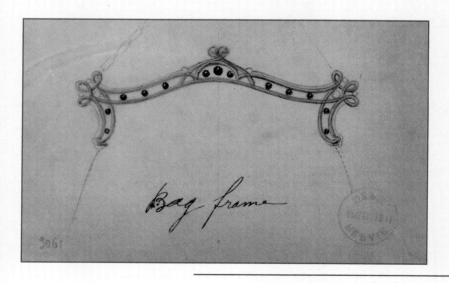

Bag frame

3061

Courtesy of the Napier Company archives.

Famed Tiffany apprentice William Rettenmeyer was employed as chief designer by The Bliss Company during the time that these creations were drawn. Courtesy of the Napier Company archives.

Stunning barefoot angel with harp featured in glass beads and a delicately jeweled frame. 8 x 11. From the collection of Diane Goldfarb. Rare.

This romantic scenic tapestry purse with a wide jeweled frame, has a peaceful pastoral scene on reverse side. 8 x 9. From the collection of Paula Higgins. $850.00 – 950.00.

This fabulous scenic may be linked with Wagner's opera, *Lohengrin*. From the collection of Marion Held. $2,000.00+.

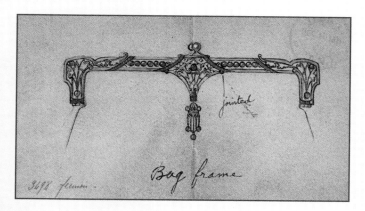

Designed on December 18, 1911, the artist's intention was for this stunning purse frame to be produced with square rubies or red jewels and an elaborate pendant drop. Courtesy of the Napier Company archives.

Elaborately sketched purse frame tipped in color made for the EA Bliss Company. Courtesy of the Napier Company archives.

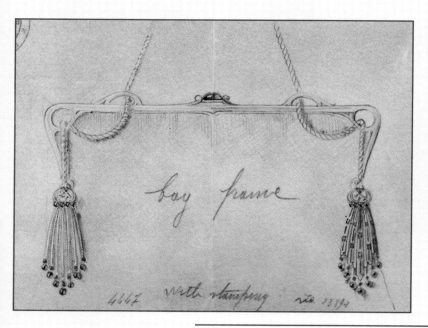

Hand-drawn and colored purse frame design with intentional variations of tassel designs. Final selection would be determined prior to the production of the piece. Dated April 16, 1913. Courtesy of the Napier Company archives.

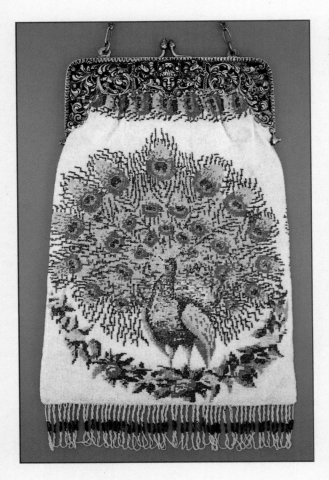

Fine glass beaded peacock figural purse of a male peafowl, distinguished by a crest of upright plumules and a greatly elongated webbed upper tail that can be erected and spread at will in a shimmering fan of many colors. Author's collection. $1,900.00+.

800 silver frame marked "Italy."

Bejeweled figural gilt purse frame; lovely figural tapestry purse with a landscape scene on the reverse. 6 x 8. The Curiosity Shop. $700.00 – 900.00.

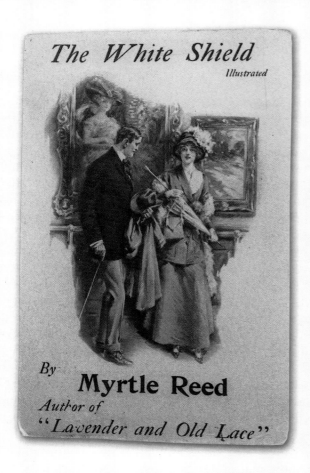

Rare figural glass beaded purse featuring an interior scene complete with furnishings and wallpaper. Elaborate peacock motif frame is decorated with genuine rubies, sapphires, and emeralds. 7½ x 12. Author's collection. Very rare.

The Delicate Art of Purse Making

A woman's purse is a most personal, yet revealing accessory. From its fundamental lines to the contents secluded within, her handbag is an aesthetic thumbprint of her personality. It may reveal a cluttered lifestyle, provide insight to ailments, or demonstrate the owner's financial acumen. But how much is known about the vintage purses our grandmothers and ancestors carried and even created? What secrets can we discover from these antiques?

It might be surprising to find that it was not the contents of these bags that do the divulging, but instead, how they are made that best tell their tales. These purses paint a tale of those who expressed themselves through their creation. Evaluation of chosen subject matter and disclosure of the materials used provide enough clarity and insight to the process that the purses themselves have become the transparencies of their lives.

As incredible as it may seem, miniscule imported hand-blown glass beads and silk thread were transformed into elaborate scenic purses. From beads carefully strung in reverse order on fine silken threads, to painstaking stitches in silk, these remarkable depictions became portable art galleries on the arms of elegant women.

Once one of these antique purses is purchased and placed safely in a collection, it's natural to wonder where it came from and how it was made. The purses themselves can even offer clues. Perhaps you recognize that the cut steel beads originated from France, or that a lining has a sewn-on label that clearly states the country of origin. But with most beaded purses it is not that simple. Designed from kits with instructions and patterns, or from pure imagination, the making of a quality vintage purse was a complex and time consuming, albeit greatly rewarding, process.

For a moment, imagine yourself many years ago, before the aid of electric light, perhaps a few slivers of waning daylight filtering through a large bay window. From your cushioned perch, you gaze over your full skirt to a basket of silk thread, often called silk purse twist, of which has been carefully chosen by the color of the dye to enhance the background color of the purse to be made. Tiny imported glass beads with small holes in them, numbering in the thousands and sold in strung clusters called hanks, now rest on the hardwood floor.

These glass gems were likely imported from Venice where skilled artisans created them by col-

A variety of beads, tassels, purses, and sundries for purse making were available in this store, founded in 1858. The specialty: Venetian beads for export.

lecting glass on a blow rod into which another rod was inserted. The glass was stretched and pulled, then roughly cut, smoothed, heated, ground, polished, and sized. A huge undertaking — all to make a tiny bead.

Of course, a very small, special needle is necessary, perhaps a handful of them because they break so easily in this tiny, fragile size — small enough to pass through the minute hole in each bead. Patience, persistence, and a touch of caution are the keys at this time. No bead hole is exactly the same size, so a few will have to be put aside if they don't easily slide through the needle on the first pass. Better not to risk breaking a delicate needle.

The frame, carefully selected for its size and intricate design, is not inexpensive. It has imported, bezel set cabochon glass stones and rests near the chatelaine on your dress. Alongside, is a shimmering piece of soft silk fabric that will later be stitched inside the purse as a lining. Spread out upon the window seat is an intricate pattern, chart, and written instructions from a specialty company that publishes information for knitting and crocheting silk bags and purses. Conveniently, these printed sheets also provide details for ordering the materials necessary to complete the project. To inexperienced eyes, the charts appear complicated, containing tiny codes and shaded areas, with glossaries indicating where to place different colors to create the desired piece. These, along with teachings passed down through generations, will provide a healthy start for the project.

Initially, the tiny beads are carefully strung, by exact color, in precisely the opposite order in which they will create the pattern. The very last bead to be placed on the precious silk thread will be the first knitted into the bag. This painstaking process might take weeks of patient sittings.

The newly adorned purse twist will be wrapped round and round small cylindrical objects for safe keeping until actually needed to create the bag. Tens of thousands of beads may be necessary to make just one knitted scenic purse. This part of the project, alone, could take months. These important ingredients, along with time, determination, and hard work, were the successful recipe for a special type of art — that which is currently considered the vintage purse.

As artistic and beautiful as some of these purses may be, those made by pious purse makers with religious

Røros Konedragt

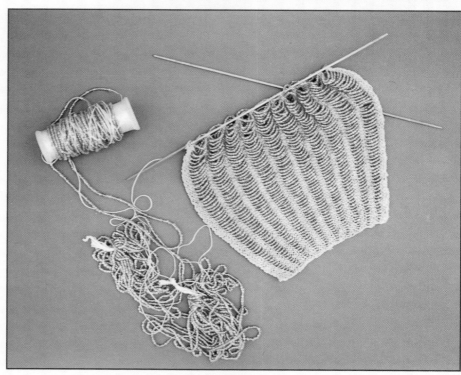

A knitted panel for an unfinished 1920s swag-style purse. This illustrates how the beads were first strung and then wrapped around a cylindrical object for safe keeping while work was in progress. The Curiosity Shop.

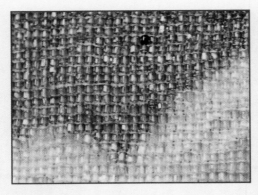

Pious purse makers often included a humility bead — a single bead, strategically placed in an area where it obviously did not belong. An intentional act, it was due to the belief that only the Almighty could create a piece of perfection. Here, you see a rounded black bead in a field of faceted blue on this canvas type glass beaded purse. 8 x 10. The Curiosity Shop. $300.00 – 500.00.

upbringings have a unique aspect. During the formation of a purse, a humility bead was purposely included. This single bead was strategically placed within the beadwork in an area where it obviously did not belong.

For example, a dark lavender bead may have been placed in the midst of a solid cream colored field of beads. If one should come across this on a purse, it is probably not a mistake. Instead, it was an intentional act, based upon the belief that only the Almighty could create perfection.

On rare occasions, purses were fashioned with a small percentage of beads purposely omitted for effect. In these select areas, only the background knitting remains. This provided the purse with an unusual, three-dimensional appear-ance; much like bags made with slightly varying bead sizes.

In the early 1800s, American "Theorem" purses were hand painted, usually on velvet, using stencils for color. After stenciling, the area was then set with a type of gum mixture. (For this form of purse to be greatly desirable today, it should be artistically well executed, and both sides should display a different scene.) Gilded brass beads could have been added for extra flavor and twisted gold wire braid might have trimmed the body of the bag in spectacular fashion. Topped with an ornate frame, this rare type of purse was surely the pride of the artist.

Needlework purses were constructed in an entirely different manner. Early twentieth century catalogs displayed an extensive selection of purse frames and various carry chains, along with canvas patterns stamped in color, with the intention of enticing the home needlepoint artisan. Adornments consisting of beads, rhinestones, powder puff cases, handbag mirrors, and miscellaneous items such as elastic, braided silk cord, loom needles, waxed bead silk, and foxtail chain were also presented for ordering ease. One could send for these canvas patterns, instructions, and all the materials needed to create the purse at home through the use of just one catalog.

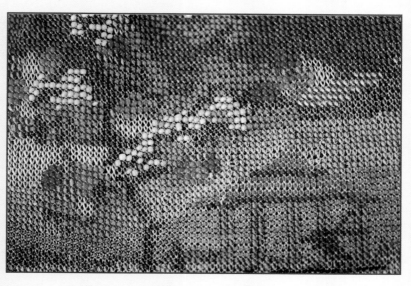

On rare occasions purses were fashioned with a small percentage of beads purposely omitted for effect. In these selected areas, only the background knitting remains, providing an unusual three-dimensional appearance. Fine glass beaded scenic. 8 x 10. The Curiosity Shop. $850.00 – 1,000.00.

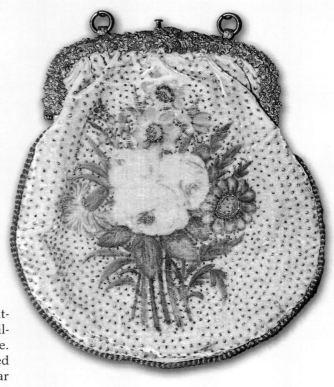

Early 1800s American-made "Theorem" purse. Hand painted on velvet with the use of stencils for color. After stenciling, the area was then set with a type of gum mixture. Gilded brass beads are added for extra flavor and twisted gold wire braid trims the body of the bag in spectacular fashion. Topped with a gold brass leaf frame, this rare type of purse was surely the pride of the artist. 8 x 10. From the collection of Paula Higgins. Very rare.

In the middle to late eighteenth century, purses from France, the Philippines, and England were made in a variety of ways, utilizing a host of materials. Wallet/purses, reticules, and misers were made from materials ranging from leather to pineapple fiber. These rare purses were fashioned using techniques that included gold and silk thread, miniscule beading with wax dipped silk or hair strands, silk embroidery, or queen stitches.

A woman in mid-eighteenth century France spent many loving hours with gold and silk thread decorating a wallet/purse with lions, hearts, and a crown. Given to a special someone, the antique French mottoes translate: "I am pleased that you find me attractive," and, "For love to be eternal, it must be beautiful."

Silk embroidered wallet/purses with unusual combinations of stags, hares, birds, insects, and butterflies were also accomplished by hand. Reminiscent of the famous wildlife embroideries worked in Boston, Massachusetts, in the eighteenth century, these designs were also popular in England.

A woman in mid-eighteenth century France spent many loving hours with gold and silk thread decorating this wallet/purse. Given to a special someone, the antique French mottoes translate: "I am pleased that you find me attractive" and "For love to be eternal, it must be beautiful." 5 x 7. From the collection of Paula Higgins. Rare.

A rare French 1780s beaded sable wallet/purse is also in evidence. Sable means "grain of sand" in French. This museum-quality piece has a reputed history of occupying a place in the collection of Charles Germain de Saint-Aubin, embroiderer to King Louis XV. Having an unusual method of assembly, beads were applied without a beading needle, as they were too fine to allow a needle to pass through the miniscule holes. Instead, silk threads dipped in wax were used. An alternative method was to tie a human hair onto the silk, threading the beads through to the silk. The beads were applied using a vertical and horizontal looping method.

Specialty shops for the affluent in Paris commissioned skilled needleworkers to create limited numbers of a variety of wallets and envelope shaped handbags to be sold as gifts. However, those with personal messages or initials were either custom finished or homemade in their entirety.

To find an antique purse that utilized queen stitches is truly a feat. The most complex of all embroidery stitches, it is also known as rococo stitch. Its use ended after the 1830s because of its difficulty to master. Simple strawberry designs utilizing difficult, intricate queen stitches were typical of the late eighteenth century.

One of the most unusual purses, by virtue of its material constitution, is an eighteenth-century knitted pineapple fiber reticule. Made in Manila, Philippines, it was exported to the European market. The entire bag, including the floral embroidery, is made of dyed pineapple fibers. The bag itself is knitted in an alternating pattern of plain

Silk embroidered wallet/purse reminiscent of wildlife appearing on the famous "Fishing Lady" embroideries worked in Boston, Massachusetts, in the eighteenth century. Rare museum piece, mid eighteenth century. 4 x 7. From the collection of Paula Higgins. Rare.

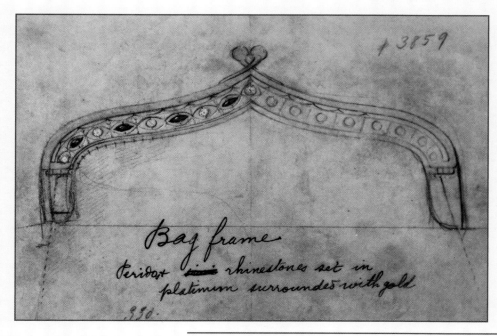

The first step in purse frame manufacture: the design. The artist intends to have peridot rhinestones set in platinum surrounded with gold. Another design idea is offered on the second half of the drawing. Courtesy of the Napier Company archives, photograph by Walter Kitik.

work — from creating a hand-painted canvas design derived from a charcoal sketch to the selection of silk colors; from intricate stitching accomplished while using a magnifying glass to the expert attachment of a purse to the frame.

Those who preferred to create beaded bags themselves in the 1920s in the United States were generally content to rely on experts who wrote booklets with suggestions in choosing purse twist (silk thread) to give their purses a unique personality. These charming homemade purses were often known as swag or paneled bags, largely because of the designs — there were no elaborate scenes or figures, just reasonably simple, pretty patterns, frequently paired with filigree or lightly jeweled frames.

Manuals with detailed instructions could conveniently be purchased in specialty shops or by mail. Editions selling for just ten cents included patterns to make over ten bags — less than a penny a purse! Illustrations of fashionable ladies holding alluring purses and jewelry filled the pages. Promising photographs of completed purses were included along with assurances of design simplicity, practical patterns, and handy bead charts. Purse assemblers could easily find bead selecting tips and other sensible advice for achieving positive results.

Homemakers were the target audience of these pattern distributors. Guides were sprinkled with advertisements for filigree and early plastic purse frames with carry chains, yarn, pure silk thread, steel crochet hooks, knitting, and sewing needles.

and diamond knit. Two other pineapple fiber purses known to be in existence are housed in museums. All are similar with only slight variations in their basket bottoms and linear floral designs.

Misers, also known as stocking purses, ring purses, double penny pouches, and long purses, could be decorated with cut steel beads, glass beads, or embroidery. They were for both men and women, though used mostly by women. The gentleman's version was generally larger and less vibrant in color. While both sexes were likely to hand carry it, a gentleman might also be inclined to place it into the pocket of his great coat, or entwine it onto his belt. On occasion, a lady might wear hers folded over a belt or hidden under her skirt.

An exquisitely netted British silk miser's purse, embroidered with sprigs of flowers is a classic miser design from the late eighteenth century. The large size, three inches by nineteen inches, also provides a clue to its age. Gilt and silver decorated sliders provided access to the slits in the pouches so that at least a few fingers could fit inside to grasp coins.

If the prospect of making a needlework or petit point purse proved to be overwhelming, there were easier ways to acquire it in the twentieth century. It could simply be purchased from an outfit that hired individual artistic talents to perform the

The bag assembly department expertly fits petit point purses to their frames.

Rare French Moroccan leather wallet with gold thread embroidery. Circa 1780 – 1790. 5 x 8. From the collection of Paula Higgins. Rare.

Fine embroidery was accomplished with the use of a magnifying glass. The embroidery is stretched into a frame and the reference pattern placed in front of the worker.

———————————

Customers were forewarned to order enough thread and beads at the onset. It was important not to run out before completing the project since dyes had a tendency to vary slightly in color from one lot to the next. Additionally, since beads were imported, there could be no guarantee that supplemental materials would match or even be accessible in the future.

Bag patterns generally required crocheting or knitting, along with beading, as part of the process. Each purse was identifiable with a name and a corresponding invoice number. The instructions were written by workers who experimented, created new designs, and literally handmade each bag prior to publication. Bead selection included imported Venetian, French Limoges, jet, coral, bone, amber, ivory, and crystal. Those with limited experience in purse making could get started by choosing from a special selection of illustrated purses that could be made by "ordinary sewing."

An excerpt from one such booklet assures the novice:

"In crocheting and knitting beaded bags, it is not a set rule to use twists the same shade as the bead used. Combinations of contrasting colors in beads and purse twist create beautiful effects. Light color beads on dark twist, or dark color beads on light twist will bring out a desired pattern more effectively than when using beads and twist which match exactly in color."

Since purse makers were encouraged to use color variations during this period, it is no wonder that many lovely swag and patterned style purses are discovered today in an array of color combinations.

Below are two purse instructions as they appeared in *A Distinctive Group of Beaded Bags,* published in 1925:

"THE TWO WIDE PANELS" Model No. D13

Materials:
29 Bunches "Hiawatha" Variegated Beads
No. 1 Spool Purse Twist
1105 or Krinkle Lustre Gyms No. 35
1 Pair "Hiawatha" Steel Knitting Pins No. 17
1 "Hiawatha" Bag Frame No. 6016/5½
1 Pair "Hiawatha" Knit Pin Protectors No. 93

Exquisite combinations can be obtained with the brilliant variegated colors of beads and blending colors of silk.

Size of bag: Width at top, 5½ inches. Length, 4½ inches.

Cast on 50 stitches. Knit back plain. Knit two more rounds or ridges to sew to frame.

Knit 3, drop a loop of fringe two inches long, knitting it into the next stitch. Continue dropping

fringe after each stitch until within 3 st of end. Knit these three plain. Knit back plain.

Knit 3, slip 2 beads, k 2, sl 2 bds, k 2, sl 2 bds, k 2, bind off next ten stitches (remembering to knit the second stitch before binding off, or you will take away one of the two you should have on the needle after the two beads are slipped) k 2, sl 2 bds, k 2, sl 2 bds, k 2, sl 2 bds, k 2, sl 2 bds, k 2, sl 2 bds, k 2, bind off next ten stitches, k 2, sl 2 bds, k 2, sl 2 bds, k 2, sl 2 bds, k 3. Knit back the same, only slip 2 inches of beads in the space where you have bound off. These 2 inches of beads suspended from one stitch to the next is best done by cutting a hem measure 2 inches long and measuring same each time, as it remains the same throughout the length of bag.

After passing about the fifteenth ridge, one bead is slipped after the first stitch on either edge and just before the last stitch on each row. (The first 15 being left off in order to have a flat surface to sew to frame sides.)

Remembering there is 1 stitch on each edge and 2 stitches on the needle between all panels or lines of beads, slip beads according to following:

American swag style 1920s glass beaded purse. A matching pattern is named "Two Wide Panels." 6 x 7. The Curiosity Shop. $225.00 – 295.00.

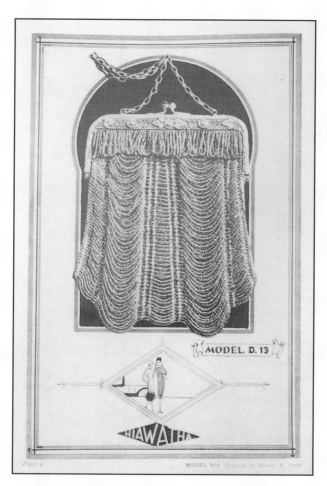

"Two Wide Panels" as illustrated in a 1925 pattern book. *A Distinctive Group of Beaded Bags*.

BEADS

3 Ridges 2. 2.2	2 Inches 2.2. 2.2.2
	2 Inches 2. 2.2
3 Ridges 2. 3.2	2 Inches 2.2. 3.2.2
	2 Inches 2. 3.2
3 Ridges 2. 4.2	2 Inches 2.2. 4.2.2
	2 Inches 2. 4.2
4 Ridges 2. 5.2	2 Inches 2.2. 5:2.2
	2 Inches 2. 5.2
5 Ridges 1.2. 6.2	2 Inches 2.2. 6.2.2
	2 Inches 2. 6.2.1
5 Ridges 1.2. 7.2	2 Inches 2.2. 7.2.2
	2 Inches 2. 7.2.1
5 Ridges 1.2. 8.2	2 Inches 2.2. 8.2.2
	2 Inches 2. 8.2.1
5 Ridges 1.2. 9.2	2 Inches 2.2. 9.2.2
	2 Inches 2. 9.2.1
5 Ridges 1.2. 10.2	2 Inches 2.2. 10.2.2
	2 Inches 2. 10. 2.1
5 Ridges 1.2. 11.2	2 Inches 2.2 11.2.2
	2 Inches 2. 11.2.1
8 Ridges 1.2. 12.2	2 Inches 2.2. 12.2.2
	2 Inches 2. 12.2.1

51 Ridges — one half of bag.

The selection of silk shades for the making of purse embroidery fell upon experienced hands.

———————

You will observe that only three panels of beads increase in width as the bag progresses, the others remaining in two's throughout the bag. Watch these widening panels to keep the beads smooth on the edges, that is, watch the space and fill it, regardless of the number of beads it takes, if they are running uneven.

"THE SIX WIDENING PANELS" Model No. D12

Materials:
20 Bunches "Hiawatha" Quality Beads No. 1525 or 43.
  1 "Hiawatha" Filigree Frame No. 5896
  1 Spool Purse Twist
  1 Pair "Hiawatha" Steel Knitting Pins No. 17
  1 Pair "Hiawatha" Knitting Pin Protectors No. 93

This fashionable bag made with six widening panels and diamonds between is exceptionally pretty when made with "Hiawatha Super-Cut" (red) beads and gray purse twist.

Size of bag: Width at top, 5 inches. Length, 5½ inches.

Cast on 44 stitches loosely. Knit back plain. Knit 2 more ridges to sew to frame. Knit 2, slip a bead, knitting it into next stitch. Continue knitting a bead into each stitch, 2 st plain on end. Knit back plain. Bead one side only for 7 ridges, coming back plain. From now on, we begin counting the ridges as 1, 2, etc., the above counting as a yoke.

Ridge 1: Knit 2, sl 1 bd, k 2, sl 1 bd, k 1, sl 1 bd, k 1, sl 1 bd, continue slipping 1 bd until you have 5 bds, then k 2, sl 1 bd, k 2, then slip 1 bd until you have 5 bds, k 2, sl 1, k 2, slip 1 bd with 1 st between until you have 5 beads. Then knit 2, slip 1 bd, and knit 2, repeating the 5 bds, etc., to end. (You should have 2 st on edge, then 1 bd, with 2 st next, then 5 bds with 1 st between giving 6 of the 1's with 2 st on either side and 5 sections with 5 beads set apart by 1 st, each.) Knit back beading only the 1 bd, and leaving off all the 5 1's.

Ridge 2: Repeat Ridge 1. (Note that each two ridges [4 rows] are just the same until you reach 17 bds in the 6 widening panels — then measuring the width of these 17, cut a hem measure and measure each time to save counting, and also make it more accurate).

Ridge 3: Knit 2, sl 2 bds, k 3, sl 1 bd, k 1, sl 1 bd, k 1, sl 1 bd, k 3, sl 2 bds, k 3, sl 1 bd, k 1, sl 1 bd, k 1, sl 1 bd, k 3, sl 2 bd, k 3, continue across slipping 3 of the one beads each in the 5 bead sections and increasing the 1 to 2 beads in the 6 panels, also increasing the stitches from 2 to 3 on either side of the widening panels. Knit back repeating the 2's and knitting plain the 8 st between.

Ridge 4: Repeat Ridge 3.

Ridge 5: Increase the 6 widening panels to 3 bds and decrease the diamonds between to 1 bead, knitting 4 st on either side of it. Knit back repeating 3's but not the diamonds.

Ridge 6: Repeat Ridge 5. Ridge 7: Goes back to 3 for diamonds and 4 slipped for the widening panels. Ridge 8: Repeat Ridge 7.

Ridges
9 & 10	5 bds for diamond and 5 for widening		
11 & 12	3	2	6 for widening
13 & 14	1	2	7 for widening
15 & 16	3	2	8 for widening
17 & 18	5	2	9 for widening
19 & 20	3	2	10 for widening
21 & 22	1	2	11 for widening
23 & 24	3	2	12 for widening
25 & 26	5	2	14 for widening
29 & 30	1	2	15 for widening
31 & 32	3	2	16 for widening
33 & 34	5	2	17 for widening
35 & 36	1	2	17 for widening
39 & 40	3	2	17 for widening
41 & 42	5	2	17 for widening
43 & 44	3	2	17 for widening
45 & 46	1	2	17 for widening
47 & 48	3	2	17 for widening
49 & 50	5	2	17 for widening
51 & 52	5	2	17 for widening

One-half of bag.

Notice the widening panels of beads are swinging loose between the stitches and beads are on both inside and outside, while the diamonds have a stitch between each bead and the beads are not repeated on the inside.

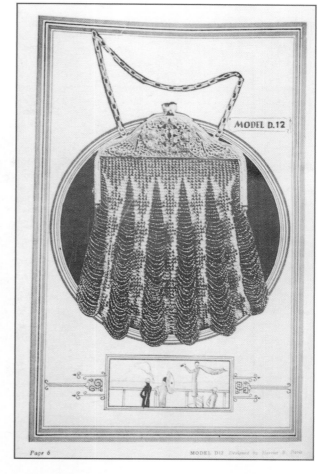

Illustration for "The Six Widening Panels," as found in a 1925 pattern instruction booklet. *A Distinctive Group of Beaded Bags.*

Entitled "The Six Widening Panels," this glass beaded purse was made in the 1920s. 6 x 7. The Curiosity Shop. $225.00 – 295.00.

Rare queen stitched wallet/purse. The most complex of all embroidery stitches, also known as rococo stitch, not in use after the 1830s. The strawberry design is typical of the era. British, circa 1790s. 4¾ x 5. From the collection of Paula Higgins. Rare.

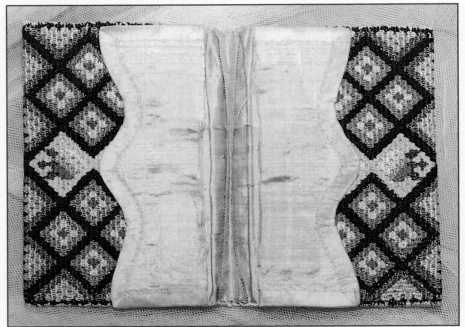

Rare French 1780s beaded sable wallet/purse. This museum quality piece has a reputed history of having a place in the collection of Charles Germain de Saint-Aubin, embroiderer to King Louis XV of France. It was made without a beading needle, as the beads were too fine to allow a needle to pass through the miniscule holes. Instead, silk threads, dipped in wax, were used. Another alternative was to tie a human hair onto the silk, threading the beads through to the silk. The beads are applied using a vertical and horizontal looping method. Made by a few specialty shops in Paris for the very wealthy. 3¾ x 6¼. From the collection of Paula Higgins. Rare.

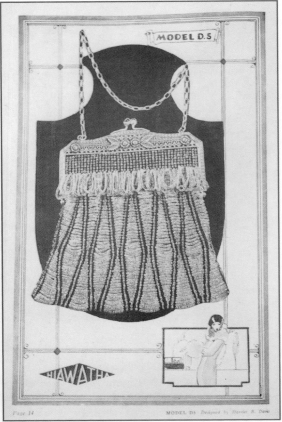

"The Single Diamond." *A Distinctive Group of Beaded Bags*, 1925.

Eighteenth century knitted pineapple fiber reticule. Made in Manila, Philippines, for export to the European market. The entire bag, including the floral embroidery, is made of dyed pineapple fibers and is knitted in an alternating pattern of plain and diamond knit. Purchased in England. Circa 1790. 7 x 9. From the collection of Paula Higgins. $600.00 – 800.00.

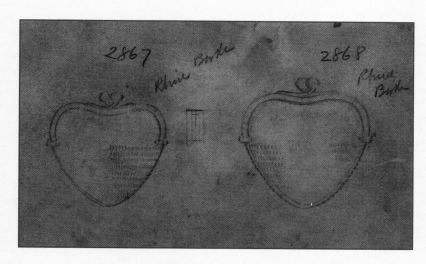

Courtesy of the Napier Company archives.

Rare British, netted silk miser's purse, embroidered with sprigs of flowers (classic miser design and length from the late eighteenth century). Gilt and silver decorated sliders for access to the pouches. 3 x 19. From the collection of Paula Higgins. $600.00 – 800.00.

I'm sending a purse full of money As a little gift to you, For if you have money on Christmas Day, You'll have it the whole year through.

427C

5532 MARGUERITE

In addition to beautiful purses inspired by famous paintings, other interesting art forms are similarly represented. Many European architectural works were transformed into scenes through glass or metal beads and stitch work on purses, as evidenced by those that include gazebos, quaint villages, mausoleums, houses, windmills, and charming cottages that are miniature masterpieces in their own right.

Castles, especially, are an appealing theme for purses and a favorite among collectors. Many Europeans took pride in their countryside, which is documented by the landscape scenic subjects of the purses they made. Germans were particularly proud of the fact that numerous exquisite castles were located in their homeland. Many of the castle purses that are seen today were duplicated primarily, although not exclusively, from these German castles, and made by those of German descent.

While innumerable castles were artistically transformed into beaded purses, there is a fascinating history behind King Ludwig II's. The Palace of Neuschwanstein, the most popular and easily recog-

nizable German castle, was ordered built in the style of the ancient German knights' castles. Commissioned in 1868, laborers toiled on its construction for nearly twenty years, between 1869 and 1886. Its elegant structural lines were later recalled on a lovely German-made purse, circa 1910. The serene setting is high above the Pollat gorge and shows the tranquil waters behind the castle along with majestic rolling mountains towering nearby.

In contrast to the balanced, peaceful surroundings, the monarch of this kingdom was rumored to have been highly eccentric. Ludwig was enthralled, nearly obsessed, with the music of Richard Wagner

King Ludwig II's castle, the Palace of Neuschwanstein, is one of the most popular and impressive German castles depicted in glass beads. Walt Disney created The Magic Kingdom in its likeness. Fine beads in glass, marked Germany. 8 x 10. The Curiosity Shop. $2,500.00 + .

and the interior was decorated accordingly. The name of the castle, Neuschwanstein, means, "new swan stone" in German. Swans, played an important role in Wagner's opera, *Lohengrin*, which was a favorite of the king. (Also a symbol of purity, they were one of his most beloved creatures).

Neither the architectural design of the fortress, nor the interior layout was approached with subtlety. Huge, ornate figural chandeliers embellished the opulent palace and a series of paintings from Wagner's opera stretched from floor to ceiling. The figural carved wood in the master bedroom, alone, took four and a half years to complete. But while the décor reverberates with bold impressive themes, the peaceful, yet equally stirring, landscape encircling the castle provides a pleasant contrast in tranquility.

Study the picture of Ludwig's castle for a moment. The style that ranges from Byzantine to Romanesque to Gothic, is not easily reproduced in beadwork. Does the distinctive mouth of an entranceway and strategically placed peaks and window openings have a familiar look to them? This is because the palace has reached icon status on American soil as Walt Disney's inspiration for the Magic Kingdom's fairytale castle. It was truly an inspiration for a beadwork enthusiast and was repeatedly reproduced in purse form.

Owning beaded purses with castle scenes was a status symbol at the turn of the twentieth century. Affluent ladies who desired to possess them would directly retain the services of a skilled bead worker. Patterns were occasionally original designs, although most of the castle bags were made from kits that these wealthy women would order and then give to the bead worker to actually make. Workers could be quite young and worked up to 14 hours a day. Higher pay was promised for faster production. Prices might be re-bartered upon completion. Money was scarce and deals were eventually struck. Smart purse makers made each bag slightly different, by variations in colors, frames, or distinctive designs so each buyer would feel that she was getting a special service.

Sometimes, these elaborate purses brought only a few dollars or were bartered for food for the bead worker's families. Many fine German shops sub-contracted work to home artisans to supply the strong demand for purses in the United States. Once the purses were sold on the retail market, new owners playfully challenged each other to guess which castle was shown on their bags.

French author Louis-Ferdinand Celine wrote, "What a picturesque residence. It's like being in operetta," in reference to another famous castle used

The Hohenzollern Palace above the Danube, situated in Sigmaringen. The oldest portion, called the keep, is visible on the purse, under the pendant drop in gray glass beads protruding from the roof of the palace like a church tower. This glorious structure was made over centuries, dating from the Middle Ages. Fine glass beads. 8 x 9. The Curiosity Shop. $2,000.00+.

as a model for a purse. Trees surround the Hohenzollern Palace above the Danube, situated in Sigmaringen, with a ledge in front of the building as it is clearly illustrated on the purse. Some castles stand freely on mountains or near the waterside with no buildings nearby. Other buildings, none of which are shown on the purse, surround Hohenzollern. While depicted accurately, it was the hardest to identify, in part because the building is slightly longer than it appears on the purse, giving it a more dramatic effect.

This glorious structure, made over centuries and dating from the Middle Ages, was not completed until the nineteenth century. The oldest and most secure portion, called the keep, which protrudes from the roof of the palace like a church tower is visible under the pendant drop in gray glass beads on the purse. The purse dates to the turn of the twentieth century.

In Germany, the Rhine River is strategically lined with many beautiful castles. On this stretch of water it was easy to collect duties, of vast impor-

Castle Stolzenfels, or Schloss Stolzenfels, spills down along the cliff-side, coming to rest at the side of the Rhine. This truly inspiring piece of pseudo-Gothic style architecture prompted the making of a very detailed and remarkable fine glass beaded purse. 8 x 10. The Curiosity Shop. $2,000.00+.

tance in the Middle Ages. The nineteenth century poet, Karl Simrock, built Parsifal House there. In his own poetic words he wrote:

"Life there will be too sweet for you, and boldness will blossom too readily in you."

It is easy to see how life could be sweet on the Rhine and how this serene area with monumental castles incited the inspiration of European purse creators.

Another castle on the Rhine is Schloss Stolzenfels, or Castle Stolzenfels. It is a truly inspiring piece of pseudo-Gothic style architecture, one that prompted the making of a very detailed and remarkable glass beaded purse. Stolzenfels lies halfway up the hillside opposite the mouth of the River Lahn, some miles above Koblenz. The famous architect Schinkel reconstructed its ruins, a gift to King Friedrich Wilhelm IV of Prussia from the people of Koblenz.

The purse shows the castle spilling down along the cliff-side, surrounded by fabulous greenery,

coming to rest at the side of the Rhine. One can only imagine the true inspiration the bead worker must have felt to spend the time to hand make this particular purse with all its detail. The small windows, the shading of the building, and the colors of nature surrounding it, all play a necessary role. Notice that the colors on the purse are true to life and not too bold. It is particularly impressive to see the great lengths to which the bead worker went in reproducing the castle on this bag. The lighter colored beads in certain sections of the castle show the effect sunlight has on the structure. Special care is also given to the chiseled peaks.

It is interesting to note that the angle of the castle depicted on the purse is not the one in which Schloss Stolzenfels was popularly depicted. Neither is it the angle depicted on the 1920s post WWI collector card marked Schloss Stolzenfels en Rhein. While positive identification has been made, these unusual conditions made the castle on the purse more of a challenge to identify, which, in turn, causes speculation as to why the bead worker would depict it from such an unusual angle. Was it a commissioned piece? And so, a mystery looms in regard to this vintage castle scenic purse.

Rhein castles date back to the Middle Ages. Looking at these beautiful purses with their unique blend of romantic and mysterious subjects, it is natural to forget the real purpose and warlike function for which the castles were built. One almost expects to see the idealistic vision of a noble knight atop his restless steed, the lovely maiden waving her handkerchief after him as he sets out on an extended journey. However, the reality of medieval times was quite contrary. Most of the castles were founded by a feuding lot and were built with preconceived notions: to protect their land from thieves and predatory neighbors, and to collect taxes.

It was the slave labor of the serfs who were forced to excavate large stones and bring them to the mountain slopes. Through sweat and toil, they fastidiously carved boulders out of the nearby landscape, thus helping to build enormous fortresses for their masters.

Forbidding mountaintops and cliffs were ideal locations for safety. A castle owner on the Rhein was able to survey the flow of traffic throughout his territory and levy tolls on German emperors who used it for frequent progresses into Italy. Rich merchants who transported their goods along the river were also taxed.

Eltz Castle, or Burg Eltz, is one of the best preserved castles in Germany, having been in the possession of only one family for centuries.

Surrounded by unspoiled land in the Eifel region, the castle is strategically located on a road that was an important route for the German Empire.

The beaded purse created in the image of Eltz Castle is more interesting than it appears at first glance. While it is detailed, it is still quite different when compared to the other castle motif purses. This castle is depicted more like a fairytale image; a bit surrealistic in soft, glowing hues. There was careful consideration given to certain fine points, especially pertaining to the coloring of the castle. Trim details also help to identify it.

The River Eltz flows around three sides of a rock crag that serves as a foundation for the castle. The unusual shapes and floor plans of the rooms are explained by the conditions of the oval crag that the inventive architects had to take into account. With such a limited area for building, the castle was made particularly high. This also explains the high peaks and clustered effect of the building's likeness shown on the purse.

Germany was not the only country that used castles as models for purse making. It was also in favor in Switzerland. There, the Chateau Chillon

The Swiss Chateau Chillon made famous by Lord Byron's poem entitled, *The Prisioner of Chillon*, rests at the very edge of picturesque Lake Geneva near Montreau. The foreboding beauty of the structure depicted in fine glass beads overshadows the dark secrets that must lurk in the depths of the castle.

Eltz Castle, or Burg Eltz, is one of the best preserved castles in Germany, having been in the possession of one family through time. A limited area for building due to rock crags explains the particularly high peaks and clustered effect of the building's likeness shown on this lovely glass beaded purse. This slightly surrealistic depiction is more like a fairytale image. 6 x 9. Author's collection. $1,800.00+.

rests at the very edge of picturesque Lake Geneva near Montreau, strategically situated by the transit road leading to Italy through the Grand-Saint-Bernard pass. Montreau, known as "Pearl of the Swiss Riviera," boasts an agreeably mild climate and miles of sheltered bays bordered by the sweet scent of flower-laden promenades.

This castle can be dated from the eleventh to thirteenth centuries, when it was rebuilt and enlarged by the joining of some 25 constructions. Documents found in archives indicate dates that work took place on the structure in the twelfth century. Originally belonging to the Bishops of Sion, it was taken over in 1536 by the Swiss who used it as a depot, an armory, and a residence for bailiffs. It was restored in the nineteenth century. Chillon is extraordinary because of its dual façade: a mountain-facing fortress and a majestic lakefront residence.

While it is characteristic to expect some romantic fable to have passed from the walls of this great castle many years ago — stories of knights, ladies, and court liaisons come to mind — however, it is quite surprising to find that, in this case, just the opposite is true. Tales of imprisonment are not quite what one would expect as motivation for creating such a spectacular beadwork purse, yet this bit of history may have played a role. It appears that the forbidding beauty of the structure itself somehow eclipsed the dark secrets that must surely have lurked in the depths of the castle; thus, the reason its magnificence was captured in glass beads.

The purse, made at the turn of the twentieth century, depicts the large rectangular walls and towers in cream colored glass beads. This effect showcases the obvious strength and stability of the landmark. One can only imagine the hopelessness of being imprisoned within these strong walls. The bead worker, so inspired by the castle, reproduced it using bold colors, softened by the blue and white tipped mountains in the background.

The fortress was made famous by a poem written in 1816 by Lord Byron entitled, *The Prisoner of Chillon*. It describes the incarceration of François de Bonnivard, a sixteenth-century French monk imprisoned by the Duke of Savoy. The Castle of Chillon and the intrigue of its famous prisoner inspired numerous poets, writers, and artists. Consequently, they poured into Montreux to set up residence.

A haunting portion describing Castle Chillon and its prison reads:

"Lake Leman lies by Chillon's walls:
A thousand feet in depth below
Its massy waters meet and flow;
Thus much the fathom-line was sent
From Chillon's snow-white battlement,
Which round about the wave inthrals:
A double dungeon wall and wave
Have made — and like a living grave
Below the surface of the lake
The dark vault lies wherein we lay:
We heard it ripple night and day;
Sounding o'er our heads it knock'd;
And I have felt the winter's spray
Wash through the bars when winds were high
And wanton in the happy sky;
And then the very rock hath rock'd,
And I have felt it shake, unshock'd,
Because I could have smiled to see
The death that would have set me free."

Castles were placed strategically, taking advantage of mountaintops or water, therefore providing the peculiar background settings of these purses. But how do we account for the mystery surrounding them? Why are their haunting stories (as with the prison of Castle Chillon) and their historical uses (such as tax collection and military defense) inducement to become romantic purse subjects? Perhaps their silent beauty has endured and overshadowed their past uses, as evidenced by true art forms found today in the remaining pieces of architecture, and in the beautiful purses reminiscent of them.

The magnificence of the Chateau Chillon in Switzerland captured in fine glass beads. Simple looped fringe, silver embossed frame with a plunger top. 8 x 10. Author's collection. $2,000.00.

A glass beaded purse with jeweled frame depicts King Ludwig II's castle, Neuschwantein. This Bavarian masterpiece was built in the style of the ancient German knights' castles, and was constructed between 1869 and 1886. 8 x 10. From the collection of Diane Goldfarb. $2,500.00 + .

Swans, like those depicted on this purse frame, played an important role in Wagner's opera, *Lohengrin*, which was a favorite of this castle's chief resident, King Ludwig II. Also, a symbol of purity, they were one of his favorite creatures. Neuschwanstein, translates to new swan stone in German. Fine glass beads. 8 x 10. From the collection of Marion Held. $2,500.00 + .

With a jeweled frame variation, this glass beaded purse displays Walt Disney's fairytale castle, otherwise known as the palace of Neuschwanstein. Unlike the balanced, peaceful surroundings of his kingdom, the monarch, King Ludwig, was reported to have been eccentric. Lavishly decorated; huge, ornate figural chandeliers and series of paintings from Wagner's opera stretched from the floor to the ceiling since the king took pleasure in his work. The purse is signed "Germany" on the interior lining. 8 x 10. From the collection of Paula Higgins. $2,500.00 + .

Lovely fine glass beaded purse with jeweled frame and rounded bottom depicting the Castle Stolzenfels. Purchased in Germany. 8 x 11. From the collection of Marion Held. $1,800.00.

Glass beaded castle scenic purse. Notice the knight riding the horse over the moor. 7 x 7. From the collection of Marion Held. $1,250.00 – 1,500.00.

Charming fine glass beaded purse scene with a castle situated at the edge of the water. Many castle scenic purses were depicted with a sailboat skimming the peaceful waters nearby. Jeweled and enameled frame, twisted loop fringe. 8 x 11. From the collection of Joyce Morgan, photograph by Harry Barth. $1,800.00+.

Glass beaded scenic in striking bold colors. Notice the detail, which includes the reflection of the tip of the castle in the water. 7½ x 10. From the collection of Joyce Morgan, photograph by Harry Barth. $1,800.00 – 2,000.00.

Made in Germany, this Alpine scenic is done in glass beads with an elaborate silver frame. 6 x 10. From the collection of Marion Held. $1,800.00 – 2,000.00.

Lovely fine glass beaded knitted castle scenic with swans, a rowboat, and a mountainous background. 8 x 11. The Curiosity Shop. $1,800.00 – 2,000.00.

A jeweled frame with shaved pearls and faceted glass stones decorates this quaint castle scenic. Notice the two observers gazing at the sailboat. Glass beads, twisted loop fringe. 7 x 11. From the collection of Diane Goldfarb. $2,000.00 + .

A castle strategically situated on a stretch of water like this, made it easier for the property owner to collect duties, which was of vast importance in the Middle Ages. Fine glass beaded purse, looped fringe, embossed frame. 8 x 10. From the collection of Joyce Morgan, photograph by Harry Barth. $1,800.00 – 2,000.00.

Castle scene depicted in hand strung fine glass beads on silk. Although it resembles Chateau l'Aigle located in Switzerland near the French border, no positive identification has been made. 7½ x 11. Author's collection. $2,000.00 + .

This charming scene captures a unique design in glass beads with unconventional flowers and foliage. Fancy lattice fringe. 8 x 11. From the collection of Joyce Morgan, photograph by Harry Barth. $1,650.00 – 1,800.00.

France, 1916.

Gorgeous tiny glass beaded purse with exotic flare. Italian mosaics made with tiny shards of glass create a floral design on the frame. 8 x 10. From the collection of Diane Goldfarb. $1,800.00 – 2,000.00.

A sobering landscape, perhaps portraying the entrance to a mausoleum. Glass beaded, floral border design, twisted loop fringe, elaborate enameled and cabochon jeweled frame. 8 x 11. The Curiosity Shop. $1,800.00 – 2,000.00.

A country landscape scene runs right through a charming floral design on this glass beaded purse. Not often seen in the foreground — an old fashioned water pump. Made in Germany, colorful twisted loop fringe. 7 x 12. Author's collection. $1,800.00 – 2,000.00.

A fine glass beaded chalet featuring a working mill. Stunning jeweled frame. 8 x 12. Author's collection. $1,800.00 – 2,000.00.

Below an elaborate jeweled frame is a lovely rose and floral design flanking a charming landscape scene. 7 x 10½. Author's collection. $1,800.00+.

A mysterious stairway is framed by luscious roses. Notice the flower basket carry chain connectors on the embossed frame. Glass beads, twisted loop fringe. 8 x 11. The Curiosity Shop. $2,000.00.

Fine glass beaded knitted purse. The frame is marked 800 silver. 8 x 12. From the collection of Joyce Morgan, photograph by Harry Barth. $1,750.00 – 1,950.00.

The same scenic pattern with a frame and color scheme variance demonstrates the difference in interpretation of the purse makers. Twisted loop fringe. 8 x 12. The Curiosity Shop. $1,750.00 – 1,950.00.

A fascinating bridge scenic. Glass beads, twisted loop fringe, embossed silver frame. 7 x 10. From the collection of Joyce Morgan, photograph by Harry Barth. $1,600.00 – 1,800.00.

A lovely jeweled frame with cabochons and figural swan carry chain connectors adorn this castle scenic purse. Plunger top. 7 x 11. From the collection of Joyce Morgan, photograph by Harry Barth. $1,700.00 – 1,900.00.

Tranquil subject on a fine glass beaded purse. Simple thumb clasp purse frame, twisted loop fringe. 7 x 11. The Curiosity Shop. $1,750.00 – 1,950.00.

A chalet is the focal point of this glass beaded purse with an enameled and jeweled frame. 6 x 8½. From the collection of Joyce Morgan, photograph by Harry Barth. $1,800.00 – 2,000.00.

A popular swan scenic purse with a red and blue enameled frame and twisted loop fringe. Pictured with a purse with the same scene but a different frame. 8 x 11. The Curiosity Shop. $1,800.00 – 2,000.00.

Glass beaded scenic purse, enameled and jeweled frame with swans. 7 x 10. Author's collection. $1,800.00 – 1,950.00.

Fine glass beaded reticule featuring a mill. Hand whipped rings, nineteenth century. 7 x 10. The Curiosity Shop. $1,650.00 – 1,850.00.

Fine glass beaded swan scenic in a bucolic setting. Glass beads, flower basket carry chain connectors. 7 x 11. The Curiosity Shop. $1,800.00 – 2,000.00.

Seagulls float overhead on this fine glass beaded purse featuring a pink edifice. 8 x 12. The Curiosity Shop. $1,850.00 – 1,950.00.

Happy New Year!

Rare fine glass beaded reticule depicts two different scenes. On one side, a lovely spring scene, on the reverse, winter. Finished with a tassel, it has a crocheted header. 7 x 11. The Curiosity Shop. Rare.

Homey scenic in fine glass beads. Made in Italy. 6 x 9. Author's collection. $1,800.00 – 2,000.00.

Fine glass beaded cottage scenic. Intricate lattice fringe. 7 x 10. From the collection of Joyce Morgan, photograph by Harry Barth. $1,800.00 – 2,000.00.

A path leads to a charming cottage in the woods. Fine glass beads, plain gilt frame with plunger top, intricate lattice fringe. 7 x 11. From the collection of Joyce Morgan, photograph by Harry Barth. $1,800.00+.

Perhaps the path will take you to the manor on the right or toward the castle silhouetted on the hill in the background. Glass beads, bright colors. 8 x 10. The Curiosity Shop. $1,850.00 – 1,950.00.

Fine glass beaded scenic purse featuring a central medallion consisting of a gazebo or mausoleum on a hill. Plunger top, gilt frame. 8 x 11. The Curiosity Shop. $1,675.00 – 1,875.00.

Charming wooded setting, rounded bottom glass beaded purse. Naturalistic colors, gilt frame with wreath pendant drop and flower basket carry chain connectors, fancy carry chain. 7 x 10. The Curiosity Shop. $1,650.00 – 1,850.00.

Micro beaded house and bridge scenic. Lovely jeweled frame with marcasite and square glass jewels. This type of frame clasp lifts and pulls back to open. 7 x 10. The Curiosity Shop. $1,750.00 – 1,950.00.

An interesting central medallion scenic purse in glass beads, surrounded by pretty blue flowers. Lightly jeweled frame, plunger top. Short lattice fringe. 7½ x 10½. From the collection of Joyce Morgan, photograph by Harry Barth. $1,850.00 – 2,000.00.

Glass beaded scenic purse of homesteads, perhaps in Holland. Wide gilded frame, swan carry chain connectors. Straight fringe ending in a loop. 6 x 9. From the collection of Marion Held. $1,750.00 – 1,950.00.

Large purse with fine glass beads and a pretty pink background. Twisted loop fringe. 10 x 11. From the collection of Marion Held. $1,650.00 – 1,850.00.

Glass beaded reticule, tassel. Crocheted header. 7 x 11. The Curiosity Shop. $650.00 – 850.00.

Farmland scenic purse, jeweled filigree frame, fine glass beads. Rounded bottom with twisted loop fringe. 7 x 10. The Curiosity Shop. $950.00 – 1,050.00.

Stunning fine glass beaded castle scenic, depicted from the vantage point of peering through grapevines. Elaborately jeweled and enameled purse frame, twisted loop fringe. This purse hung in the Hobe office for many years before it was acquired from their estate. 8 x 12. Author's collection. Rare.

Going Away.

Copyright, Leslie Judge Co., N. Y.

Fine glass beaded castle mountaintop scenic purse. Simple frame, twisted loop fringe. 6 x 9. The Curiosity Shop. $1,650.00 – 1,850.00.

Twin houses are the focal point of this medium glass beaded loomed purse. Simple straight fringe. 8 x 10. The Curiosity Shop. $395.00 – 495.00.

Windmill scenic purse, lattice fringe, glass beads. 7 x 11. From the collection of Joyce Morgan, photograph by Harry Barth. $950.00 – 1,150.00.

Glass beaded purse. Nicely executed with details including a reflection appearing in the water. 8 x 10. The Curiosity Shop. $950.00 – 1,200.00.

Fine glass beaded purse in popular design with a colorful twisted loop fringe, jeweled frame with flower basket pendant drop and swan carry chain connectors. This purse was also produced with a different frame in a smaller size. 8 x 12. From the collection of Diane Goldfarb. $1,400.00 – 1,600.00.

Scenic purse with lovely marcasite and carnelian jeweled frame. This purse design was also made in a larger version. Twisted loop fringe, glass beads. 6 x 9. The Curiosity Shop. $1,300.00 – 1,500.00.

Fine glass beaded castle scenic purse with jeweled frame. The twisted loop fringe is tipped in purple. 8 x 11. The Curiosity Shop. $1,400.00 + .

Glass beaded figural purse with charming gazebo and foliage. An innovative flower basket design with spilled roses covers the entire frame. The reverse has another scene depicting a girl and lamb near a weeping willow. 6 x 7. From the collection of Marion Held. Rare.

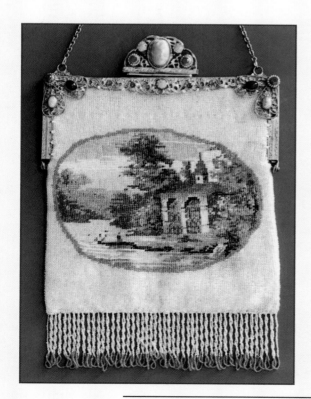

Fine glass beaded purse with scenic medallion depicting a structure with large open arches. Ornate jeweled frame with filigree work. 6 x 9. The Curiosity Shop. $1,250.00 – 1,450.00.

A Venetian scenic fine glass beaded purse features a gondola, bridge, and an apron adorned woman walking nearby. 7 x 9. From the collection of Paula Higgins. Rare.

Lovely fine glass beaded scenic. A diamond pattern surrounds the central focal point. Enameled frame, twisted loop fringe. 7 x 11. The Curiosity Shop. $1,400.00 – 1,600.00.

Made in Germany, an expansive castle spills over a hill to the waterside. Jeweled frame, twisted loop fringe. 7 x 10½. Author's collection. Rare.

Glass beaded scenic purse of gazebo and castle on a hill. This particular design has appeared many times in scenic purses. 8 x 12. The Curiosity Shop. $1,450.00 – 1,600.00.

This medium beaded castle scene includes details such as the reflective tip of the castle in water and a meandering path to a charming home. A loomed bag with twisted looped fringe and a simple frame. 7 x 11. The Curiosity Shop. $1,250.00 – 1,450.00.

1909.

Structures loom in the distance on this lovely nineteenth century glass beaded purse. 6 x 8. From the collection of Marion Held. $1,250.00 – 1,450.00.

Foliage decorates the bottom of this glass beaded scenic with jeweled frame. 8 x 10. The Curiosity Shop. $1,250.00 – 1,450.00.

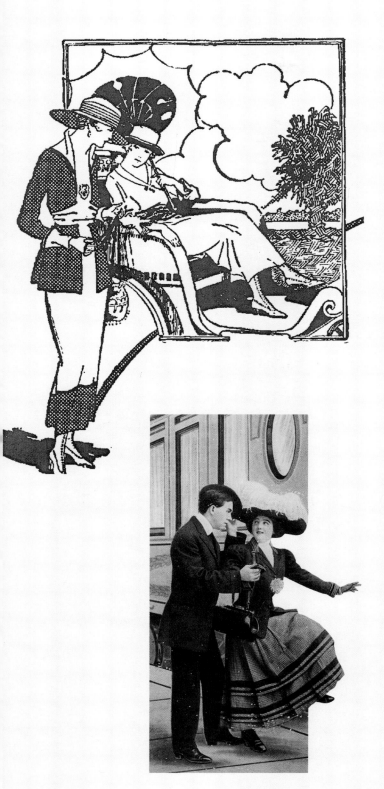

Circa 1910.

The small size and fine glass beads add to the charm of this scenic purse that includes an enchanting gazebo on a hillside and a mysterious tunnel beneath it. 6 x 9. The Curiosity Shop. $1,250.00 – 1,450.00.

With a solid color beaded background, this purse depicts a building surrounded by flowers and foliage. 6 x 10. The Curiosity Shop. $1,200.00 – 1,400.00.

This serene area with monumental castles incited the motivation of European purse creators. Known as the palace of Neuschwanstein, owned by King Ludwig II, it was later inspiration for Walt Disney's Magic Kingdom. 8 x 10. Author's collection. $2,500.00+.

6 x 9. The Curiosity Shop. $650.00 – 950.00.

Fine glass beaded reticule with a crocheted header and twisted looped fringe in a variety of colors. Notice the deer on the bottom portion of the purse. Nineteenth century. 6 x 10. The Curiosity Shop. $1,000.00 – 1,200.00.

In the Middle Ages knights wore entire outfits made of durable ring or chain mail mesh, including facemasks, gloves, and boots, for protection in battle. Metal workers who made these suits of armor, a form of artwork in its own right, could work up to three years making a single suit. An ancient tunic, alone, presently housed in the Metropolitan Museum of Art, contains nearly a quarter of a million hand-made and tempered rings that were carefully formed and sep-arately riveted.

Unlike the efficient, machined manufacture of mesh purses in the past century, the early chain mail and ring mesh workers, if they were so inclined, would have taken weeks to create a single hand-made mesh purse using the primitive materials and tools available at that time.

Bezel set cabochons, faceted stones, and shaved pearls decorate this exquisite Art Nouveau, jeweled moth motif mesh link purse. 7 x 11. Author's collection. Very rare.

To comprehend just how long it took using this antiquated technique, it should be understood that the lengthy process began with each piece hammered into a round state from thin strips of iron. Then the chain mail was cut with a chisel, with the ends overlapping. Again, it was hammered, this time until flat, and then, finally riveted together. An armorer might labori-ously make and weave together approximately 250 links in a lengthy workday.

Chain mail mesh was in use prior to the Middle Ages, as evi-denced by depictions of Egyptian and Greek soldiers wearing it in battle. Although it would be difficult to determine exactly when the first mesh purses were made, the earliest indication points to those made of gunmetal during the late 1700s.

Through the centuries, mesh has evolved from a man's nec-essary protective garment to a woman's fashion accoutrement. But it wasn't until the nineteenth century that these purses increased in popularity among well-dressed, fashion-savvy women. If there was monetary means for a stylish hat and prop-er gloves, there was always room for a sparkling metal mesh purse to complement the outfit. Ready to dangle from a chate-laine, wrist, or pinkie, this accessory helped to make the lady a stately sight.

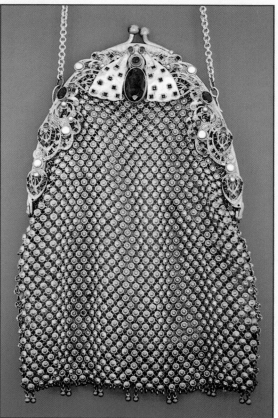

An ornate wide frame embellished with jewels and cherubs crowns a square linked mesh purse. The mesh forms a distinct pattern on the bag. Hinged frame handle, suitable for attaching to a belt or chatelaine. 7 x 10. Author's collection. Rare.

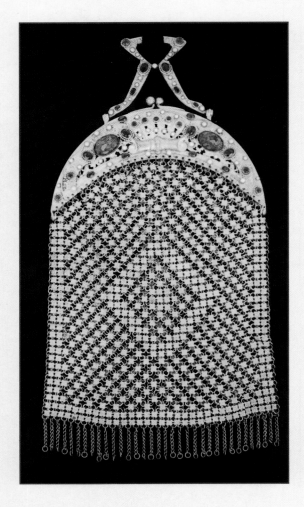

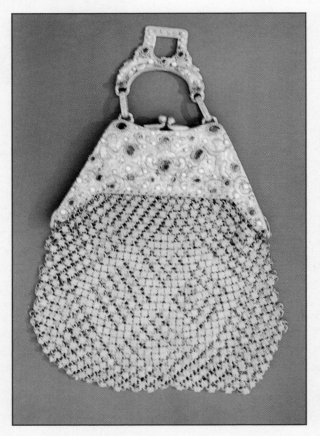

Stunning mesh link purse with ornate faux lapis jeweled frame and finger ring holder. 7 x 11. Author's collection. Rare.

Early production methods required a company to sub-contract for ring mesh assembly. Mesh was linked together in private homes, with workers being compensated upon completion of the job. Later, an automatic machine was invented to produce mesh for more expeditious purse assembly.

In the 1800s mesh chatelaine purses were highly favored. They were usually German silver, silver plated, gunmetal, sterling, or 800 silver, with a central ring on the carry chain for ease in attaching to a chatelaine. During this period, magazines and newspapers offered other German silver and silver-plated mesh bags as a premium free of charge in exchange for the sale of new subscriptions.

Sometimes frames were elaborately cast or stamped with designs of snakes, cherubs, and similarly interesting images. Others featured ladies with flowing hair and flowers that contained an unmistakable Art Nouveau influence. Often, metal beads and elongated drops were attached to the bottom of the purse for adornment. The popularity of these types of mesh bags continued until the turn of the twentieth century.

Obviously, mesh was hardly a new material when it was manufactured for purses in the early twentieth century although this is when the most popular mesh bags began to emerge.

German silver mesh purse with embossed frame and drops. 6 x 6. The Curiosity Shop. $125.00 – 200.00.

The Whiting and Davis Company and Mandalian Manufacturing Company were recognized as the most prevalent mesh manufacturers of this era. This was due not only to the enormous amount of purses each produced (although Mandalian's tenure was shorter lived) but also because of their exposure through advertising. It was especially true in the case of the Whiting and Davis Company. The Napier Company (formerly E.A. Bliss Company), Evans Manufacturing Company, the R&G Company, and some lesser known European and American companies, also manufactured mesh purses during this period.

In 1875, the soon-to-become Bliss/Napier Company was started with the partnership of two men, surnamed Whitney and Rice, in North Attleboro, Massachusetts. At the onset, items manufactured were predominantly men's watch chains and small gifts. Sales agent Edgerton Ames Bliss in conjunction with a man named Carpenter, envisioned a great future in jewelry and novelties. They agreed to purchase the company in 1882, and the name was changed to Carpenter and Bliss. It was soon evident that thirty-three year old Bliss was becoming the active head of

Baby mesh enameled purse by Whiting and Davis. Heavy frame with unusual interior clasp mechanism. An extremely rare colorful figural purse featuring a lady with fan being courted by a gentleman with mandolin. Lined. 8 x 5½. Author's collection. Very rare.

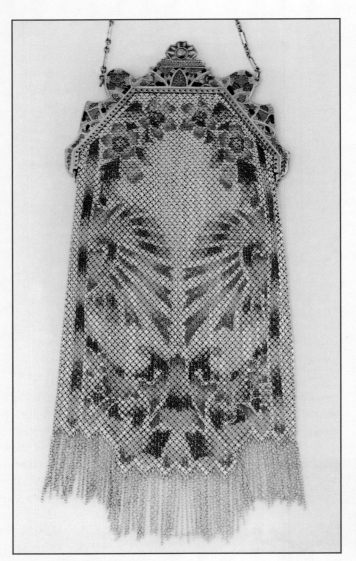

A bright and colorful Mandalian Manufacturing Company enameled mesh purse utilizing baby mesh. Extra fancy enameled frame, sometimes referred to as "stained glass" because of the small metal pockets filled with colored enamel. Lined. Unusually long, measuring 4½ x 10½. Author's collection. Rare.

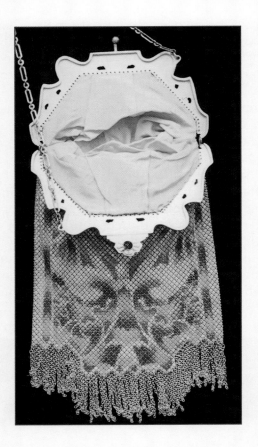

the fledgling company. In July of that year, Carpenter retired and the company was incorporated as the E.A. Bliss Company.

The new management began with a larger offering of goods that included purses. Originally from New York, Bliss opened an office there. To keep current on Parisian fashions, he traveled extensively to Europe where he purchased stones and beads used to accentuate purse frames and manufacture jewelry. Ambitious and savvy, the company owed much of its success to his untiring efforts.

To acquire larger working quarters, the main factory was moved to Meriden, Connecticut, in 1893. The building was an old ivy-covered brick flint glass factory, one of the first ornamental glass producing plants in the country. Bliss hired William R. Rettenmeyer, who was credited with an apprenticeship in silversmithing from the re-known Tiffany and Company, as the new chief designer and stylist. E.A.

Despite all the thick petticoats, corsets, stylish hats, and proper gloves, there was always room for one more accessory to complement the outfit — a glimmering metal mesh purse!

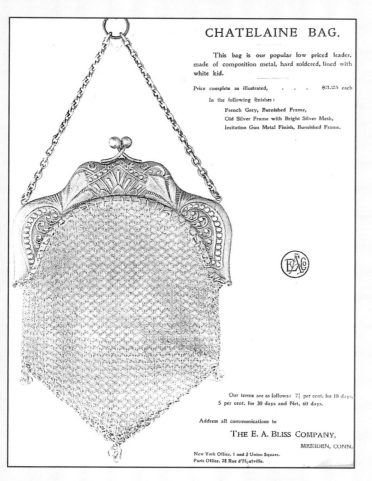

CHATELAINE BAG.

This bag is our popular low priced leader, made of composition metal, hard soldered, lined with white kid.

Price complete as illustrated, . . . $3.25 each

In the following finishes:

French Grey, Burnished Frame,
Old Silver Frame with Bright Silver Mesh,
Imitation Gun Metal Finish, Burnished Frame.

Our terms are as follows: 7½ per cent. for 10 days,
5 per cent. for 30 days and Net, 60 days.

Address all communications to

THE E. A. BLISS COMPANY,
MERIDEN, CONN.

New York Office, 1 and 3 Union Square.
Paris Office, 28 Rue d'Hauteville.

Mesh chatelaine purses were highly favored in the 1800s and continued their popularity into the 1900s. This advertisement for the E.A. Bliss Company depicts a chatelaine purse made of composition metal, soldered, and lined with white kid for $3.25. Courtesy of the Napier Company archives.

Bliss was the first to manufacture sterling silver giftware and novelties in Meriden and the company was one of the most prosperous in the area. Their product line was varied with jewelry and giftware, including match safes, sterling silver bonnet brushes, silver buckles, ornate manicure and stationery articles, fancy handled shoe horns and buttonhooks, sterling lorgnettes, elaborate silver trays, and lovely chatelaine purses. Launching an advertising campaign to reach quality retailers, they became a large supplier to fine jewelry and department stores.

The fashion jewelry and accessories they offered grew in favor with well-dressed gentlemen and ladies of the day. In the early 1900s, the New York office was moved to the hub of the retail business center: Fifth Avenue. Rettenmeyer's son, Frederick, joined the force in 1907. The trademark during these early years consisted of "EA Co" in script, with the imprint of a bee in flight, set inside a circle. This mark can be found stamped inside purse frames made during this period.

Chatelaine purses and handkerchief pockets were of ring or flat (armor plate) mesh made from a variety of materials including white metal, gunmetal, silver, and nickel silver. Many were lined with kid leather. A metal soldered purse, lined with white kid leather, was offered for just $3.25. Finishes on purse frames included French gray burnished, old silver and imitation gunmetal. Mesh could be had in quadruple plate, silver, gunmetal, or glazed in Roman gold, bright silver, satin, or old silver. Ornate fittings could also be purchased separately.

Edgerton Bliss died suddenly in Massachusetts at the age of sixty-two. His son, William E. Bliss, vice president of the company, became the acting head soon after his father's death.

In 1919, the company introduced a fine mesh bag called Nile-Gold that was available with variations in the frame design. By advertising it in wholesale trade publications they were able to reach retail distributors who purchased in quantity. National advertisements were assigned to first-rate publications like *Vogue* and *The Red Book*.

The company trademark was again changed, this time to a rectangular block with the word "BLISS" inside. In 1920, James Napier was elected president and general manager. In recognition of his work in the growth and revitalization of the business, the name of the company was changed to the Napier-Bliss Company.

In 1923, the business name was finally changed to the Napier Company. Many of the mesh purse frames made during this period are recognizable chiefly because of their noticeably longer jaws. Over the years the company continued to grow, opening sales offices in Chicago, Texas, and Los Angeles. In 1960, James Napier died and Frederick Rettenmeyer was elected president. The Napier Company ceased operations in 1999 after more than a century of production.

In 1876, William H. Wade and Edward P. Davis founded a jewelry factory called the Wade Davis Company, in Plainville, Massachusetts. With great determination, a young office helper by the name of Charles A. Whiting was incrementally promoted from his nine cents per hour position to become one of the best New York sales managers. He became a partner while still in his twenties. Sixteen years later, in 1896, he and Davis raised enough capital to purchase the company. They changed the name to the Whiting & Davis Company and introduced mesh purses. In 1907, Whiting purchased Davis's interest, becoming president and treasurer while keeping the name of the prospering company as a tribute to his loyal former partner.

Initially, the bags were made by hand, and the work was laborious. A finished product ready for the marketplace took time. Meanwhile, demand was steadily increasing. Whiting needed a significantly faster, more efficient method of manufacturing mesh. Then, in 1912, A.C.

Small gunmetal purse. A loop in back allows for attachment to a chatelaine. 2½ x 3. The Curiosity Shop. $95.00 – 175.00.

Fabulous baby enameled mesh Mandalian with enameled frame and colorful scene depicting an ornamental vase overflowing with flowers. Lined. 4½ x 10. Author's collection. $1,500.00+.

History shows that mesh evolved from a protective garment before the Middle Ages, to a fashion statement, becoming a virtually necessary luxury!

Pratt invented the world's first automatic mesh machine. Anticipating its importance, Whiting and Davis purchased the patent, becoming the first to benefit from this new innovation. The machinery increased the production of mesh bags enormously. In conjunction with the growing volume, the company launched a major nationwide advertising campaign. This brilliant strategy vaulted the company to success, as it became the largest purse manufacturer in the world.

Keeping costs down by producing in quantity, the company was capable of creating a fast selling product for the average person. Year-round advertising was intensified prior to holidays and seasonal events. Whiting's sales experience elevated the company to new heights.

By 1922, in order to keep up with the demand for his purses, Whiting had a branch factory in Quebec, Canada, a New York office on Fifth Avenue, and a Chicago branch, in addition to their factory headquarters in Massachusetts. He kept a staff of 50 engineers and mechanics who developed and registered numerous additional patents. Nearly all of the hundreds of new mesh-making machines were constructed in their own plants. The firm was the first to use solder-filled wire in the making of metal mesh. A busy network of automated machinery spun bars of solid metal into threads of gold and silver. The threads were woven into many patterns and shapes, all to become mesh bags. Links were made and woven with such quick precision that the process hummed along at the unbelievable rate of 600 to 700 rings per minute, per machine!

Over 200,000 mesh rings might be needed for a single purse, each soldered simultaneously. When it was placed in an electric furnace, the thin trace of solder melted and flowed. The mesh body was joined to the frame using one fine spiral wire in a method called "hanging up." This innovation was improved from the inferior, time-consuming process of connecting body to frame with separate links. The Whiting and Davis insignia was impressed on the metal purse frame or attached with a small metal tag hung on the interior of the bag.

Soldered and unsoldered varieties included fine ring and flat link mesh. Fine ring mesh was also called baby ring mesh, or simply fine mesh. Sunset mesh was the name given to a colorful treatment that alternated in gold, bronze, and brass stripes on fine ring mesh.

Single tiles or links are sometimes referred to as the spider or armor mesh, but are most often called flat links. These links consist of a small piece of flat metal plate in the shape of a diamond with four tiny "arms" at each point. The arms were used to connect to a small metal ring at each corner by bending the arm into the ring. When this was done repeatedly, it created a flat surface. High-speed presses punched

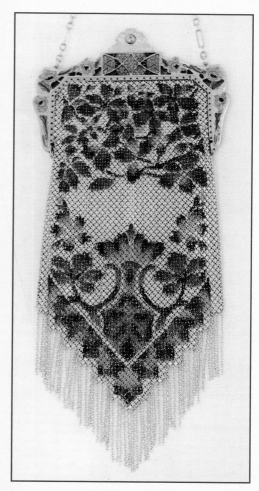

Mandalian enameled mesh purse with floral decoration. Pretty floral enameled matching frame and goldtone fringe. 4 x 10. Author's collection. $800.00 – 1,000.00.

Rows of mesh making machinery, able to transform metal into mesh links at the rate of 700 per minute. Courtesy of the Napier Company archives.

Fabulous Mandalian baby mesh purse with sterling enameled frame. 4 x 10. The Curiosity Shop. $1,200.00+.

out a large number of links and rings. They were individually woven into long sleeves of mesh fabric, then cut and sized.

Early in the decade, Whiting and Davis mesh purses were of sterling silver, 14-karat gold, 18-karat gold plate, silver plate, or gunmetal and have a fine, silky texture. These bags do not have colored enamel, so alluring designs had to be created through variations in frame shapes and embossing, mesh straps, and a variety of unusual mesh decorations. These decorations were given names such as Venetian (a floral shaped mesh insert just above the fringe), Egyptian (chain linked fringe with pointed peaks) and Bacchus (even chain link fringe).

The production of colorful fine mesh Dresden bags began in the 1920s. The name was derived from the German inventor who developed the machine. Made with a colored silk-screened process, giving the bag a surrealistic watercolor appearance, these purses are especially vibrant.

Flat mesh purse links were colored by enameling. Patterns and colors were plentiful and varied. Enameled designs were made in different color schemes providing collectors with incentive to get a patterned mesh purse in every conceivable color combination.

Another type of flat mesh is called beadlite. It has a raised metal dot in the center of the link, giving it a three-dimensional look. When colored enameled is added, it mimics the ever-popular beaded bag.

The Princess Mary manufactured by this company appeared to have an envelope-shaped body when the unique flap over top was closed. The purse was named after the royal sister to Edward VIII and King George VI of England who, in a highly publicized wedding, married the sixth Earl of Harwood in 1922. It was available in goldtone or silvertone fine ring mesh, Sunset mesh, or flat enameled mesh. There is also a fancy flat mesh design with a color-

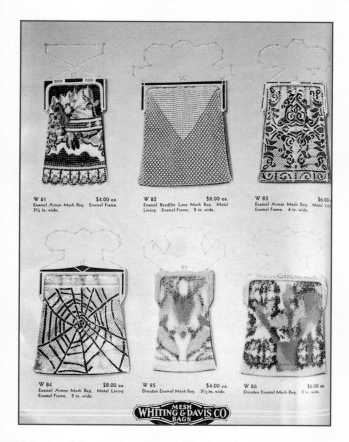

Whiting and Davis Company. *The Jeweler's Circular*, 1931.

ful rose depicted in the center of the outside flap, and another that has an applied enameled floral medallion in the same vicinity.

Whiting and Davis also sold El-Sah bags. These bags have an additional metal tag attached on the inside or a logo impressed into the frame's interior. They were made from a variety of patterns but have no overall distinguishing features, except in the case of the El-Sah vanity bag (compact purse) that is highly desirous today.

Several types of Whiting and Davis bags were not known by specific names but still have distinguishing features that set them apart from the rest. For instance, purses with a widely flared mesh skirt were originally priced between $15 and $18. The level of expertise and the amount of material used to manufacture these was greater than that of their average-sized brethren. These purses were manufactured in flat enameled mesh and beadlite.

The Whiting and Davis Company had an innovation commonly known as a "scis-

sors style" purse because of the wide opening/crossover effect accomplished by opening the large frame jaws. It is made in silver tone or gold tone and constructed only in supple fine baby mesh.

Additionally, this company made a gold tone, gate-top ring mesh purse. The frame is alternatively referred to as "accordion style," because of the ability of its neck to expand allowing access to the interior of the purse. The flexible joints are manufactured with hinged metal strips resembling latticework. A plain, enameled, or jeweled lid snaps atop the purse when the neck is pushed close. Carry chains were sometimes attached to a chatelaine style hook.

Prospective wholesale clients would embark on a special buying trip to the Whiting and Davis Company to view purses like these before faithfully stocking store shelves and showcases with them. This enabled them to examine an exclusive line or purchase in quantity to secure a volume price. The factory provided motor cars to meet visitors in Boston, Massachusetts, or Providence, Rhode Island, wherever it was reasonably convenient. Important potential customers, with limousine service and a company driver at their disposal, were then transported to the Plainville factory to begin their excursions. Tours began with a peek at Charles Whiting's private office, appointed with hard wood flooring, raised wood paneled walls and a roll top desk on which a free standing telephone with a fixed receiver and separate earpiece was kept.

Next, the visitor was able to get a glimpse of the factory and the all-important mesh-making machinery located in a large department. Here, the customer could view firsthand the manufacturing techniques and equipment in the plant. The ceiling was virtually covered with columns of silver loom-

The Whiting and Davis Company in Plainville, Massachusetts.

ing overhead. Production was orderly and hardwood floors were kept clean. In the room was a panorama of spools, wires, and wheels. Row after row of machines transformed round columns of silver into delicately woven and nearly transparent luminous silver thread used in the making of mesh links. In the assembly room, trained laborers sat on benches working with precision tools and jets of gas flame. Day after day they soldered joints and ball knobs onto purse frames. Highly skilled artisans performed decorative detailing, including engraving and hand setting imitation gems. Frames were impressed with Whiting and Davis trademarks.

A deal was imminent when the wholesaler was escorted to the visitor's dining room that was part of the factory. Furnishings were sparse but comfortable, structured to promote socialization. Mr. Whiting, who was rarely known to dine alone, played the host at noon, offering wholesome and simple New England cooking. Modestly describing the company's dining area, the public relations department wrote: "This little nook is very plain, very quiet, but very convenient in a little town more famous for mesh bags than for restaurants."

Once the transaction was completed and the

wholesale distributor purchased Whiting and Davis purses, the business genius behind the company did everything to ensure the success of his customer. Backed by a huge marketing campaign in 1922, ads were placed on a monthly basis in magazines like *Delineator*, *Vogue*, *Harper's* and *Ladies' Home Journal*. The Whiting and Davis promise was: "From the pages of these magazines, they will step into your store."

As a part of this gesture, the company would repair any of the bags they manufactured, regardless of condition, for a fraction of the original cost. They guaranteed durability and dependability and supported this by maintaining a service department located in a special section of the plant. Service was performed free of charge in the event that a bag had accidental damage. Purses were washed, polished, and could be re-plated if necessary. Within two or three weeks they were re-assembled to original specifications.

Mesh purses by Whiting and Davis had become such an integral part of women's fashion that there was a constant demand for new patterns. Company representatives kept a constant vigil on the world of fashion in Paris and New York, thus enabling the company to anticipate any major movements in the ever-changing world of fashion. French designer, Paul Poiret, gained attention when he banned the use of restrictive corsets in women's wear. Utilizing his celebrity status, he was paid substantial royalties for his endorsement of the Parisian inspired Whiting and Davis purse carrying his namesake in the mid-twenties. Poiret Pouch Shape Costume Bags were

Dresden style mesh purses by the Whiting and Davis Company. The purse on the left is meant to look like roses measuring 5 x 6; on the right 3½ x 6. From the collection of Paula Higgins. $325.00 – 450.00 each.

framed, silk lined, and available in a variety of colors. Found in exclusive jewelry shops, the most distinctive feature of the bag is the widening toward the bottom into a traditional pouch shape.

In 1938, Whiting's grandson, Charles Whiting Rice, began working for the company. When Rice arrived, the product line had already changed from colorful enameled mesh bags to solid gold or silver colored bags. Two years later, Charles Whiting died at the age of seventy-six. Charles Rice became vice president of the company.

Shortly before World War II, the company introduced a new style of mesh bag. Called Alu-mesh, it was a white summer bag with large mesh links that sold in the price range of $4.95 to $7.95. Typically, frames were made of an early plastic. Material with both the style names and the Whiting and Davis logo was sewn into the lining of the bag. At their peak, 600,000 of these bags were made within a year.

In 1960, Charles Rice became president of the company that his renowned grandfather helped to make so prosperous. He retired six years later, in 1966, after the company was sold to Certified Pharmaceuticals.

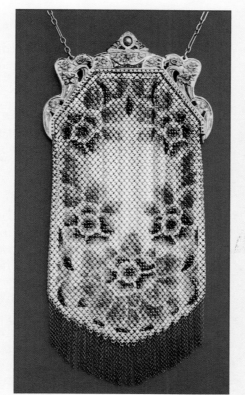

Mandalian enameled mesh purse in a floral design. Pierced openwork floral enamel frame design. 4 x 10. From the collection of Elaine Lehn. $700.00 – 900.00.

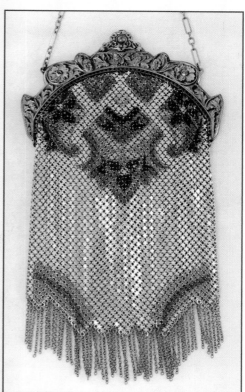

Enameled mesh purse by Mandalian with deeply embossed arched frame. Colorful rainbow type design. 4 x 9. The Curiosity Shop. $550.00 – 750.00.

Evans Company vanity purse. The lid opens to reveal powder, mirror, and powder puff. Goldtone flat mesh body. 3 x 6. The Curiosity Shop. $225.00 – 375.00.

Today, the Whiting and Davis Company Safety Division continues to produce mesh apparel from the same types of materials that were used centuries ago by knights as protective armor in battle.

Shark proof diving suits, metal safety gloves and aprons, for the meat cutting industry, sleeves, arm guards, chest protectors, chaps, and even full-body tunics are solid sellers made from stainless steel ring mesh.

The Whiting and Davis Company's primary competitor was a man named Sahatiel Garabed Mandalian. Born in Armenia, Turkey, in 1869, he was the founder of what was to become the Mandalian Manufacturing Company, famous for making high quality mesh purses. At the age of 20, he emigrated to the United States in 1889 and moved to North Attleborough, Massachusetts. He attended the Rhode Island School of Design. Once settled in America, he met and married Lillian Green Fuller in 1903.

Early in his business career he formed a company called Casper and Mandalian. At the onset, their firm was primarily engaged in the manufacture of jewelry cufflinks and novelties, and had not as yet emphasized mesh bags.

Eugene A. Hawkins replaced Mr. Casper in 1906, and the firm became known as Mandalian and Hawkins. During this time the company began extensive production of mesh purses and was well respected throughout the area.

of imitation pearls. The trademarked name was imprinted on celluloid and paper tags as well as on boxes. Some of these mesh bags can still be found in their original boxes especially if they were given as special gifts, cherished and tucked away in a safe place for years. Purses discovered with these extras add to their value.

Bags made by Mandalian differed from those made by his primary competitor, Whiting & Davis, in many ways. Mandalian designs were chiefly florals influenced by the Victorian era or Near Eastern carpet patterns reminding him of his native homeland. Other designs were naturalistic depictions of creatures, such as birds and butterflies. Jeweled and enameled frames were combined with enameled flat mesh. Ornate frames with stamped openwork and elaborate etching were also used. At times, extra fancy enameled frames were produced with a technique sometimes referred to as "stained glass." In this case, shallow metal pockets in irregular shapes were formed and filled with various colored enamel. Mandalian pioneered the use of metal drops instead of chain link fringe to create a dramatic finish. Bags can sometimes contain an original silk lining with

In 1921, this enameled mesh black and white tapestry design purse was the first offered color by the Whiting and Davis Company. 3 x 8. The Curiosity Shop. $295.00 – 495.00.

Mesh bags were manufactured under the name of Mandalian and Hawkins until 1915 when Mandalian purchased Hawkin's interest. The firm's name was changed to the Mandalian Manufacturing Company and was stamped accordingly on the inside of the metal frames. Sahatiel foresaw the potential in the mesh industry and began a full-fledged effort to create highly desirable and aesthetic bags. The first fish-scale mesh machine was invented and perfected under his supervision. It was a secret process, producing an unusual glow on furnace-fired enameled links, known as Lustro-pearl, fish-scale mesh, or pearlized mesh. Made from a compound of fish scales purchased in large quantity from the fisheries on Cape Cod, its effect was similar to that produced by jewelers in the manufacture

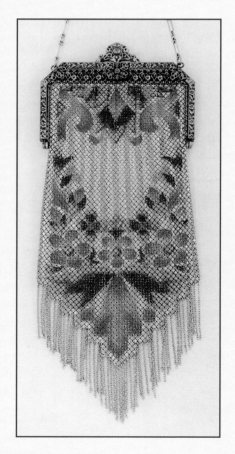

Fancy Mandalian enameled mesh purse with a striped design and a pleasant pink, red, and teal color combination. 4 x 9½. Author's collection. Rare.

tiny pockets sewn into them. If luck prevails, a beveled glass mirror can still be found in the pocket of the lining.

The Mandalian Company produced a specialty feature called baby mesh or petit flat (armor) mesh. This distinct mesh had links of about half the average size. It was more difficult to enamel and took longer to manufacture, but it yielded a more desirable product. Smaller links allowed for a more supple sensation during handling. Baby mesh was usually made into larger, superior quality bags that were more expensive. Special care was given to the frames that were wired to these kinds of mesh bags. Although the Whiting and Davis Company also produced baby mesh links in manufacturing, it is more often found on Mandalians.

Mandalian produced some very interesting styles, including The Martha Washington purse. The bag was designed to emulate the brown satin ribbon work embroidered reticule that the famous first lady made and held during George Washington's inauguration in 1789. Unusual in its composition, this purse had an enameled mesh body with a fabric reticule header attached. The purse was accessed with a draw closure. These closures consisted of fabric cord or metal chain and could be decorated with finger rings or filigree balls. The mesh portion of Martha Washington purses is furnished with either chain fringe or metal drops.

Mandalian also manufactured the Gloria Bag. The most distinguishing feature of this purse is the unique jointed frame referred to as "bracelet style." These independent links are banded together with a series of springs to form a frame. When the clasp at the top is closed, the frame is stationary; when opened, the mouth of the purse takes on the shape of a circle to allow entry into the bag.

The production philosophy of the Whiting & Davis Company was to concentrate chiefly on geometric and deco designs, along with some figurals — the emphasis clearly on creating an affordable product for the masses. However, Whiting and Davis also made some very interesting vanity bags and novelty purses. In one case, an esoteric purse has a single large glass jewel — not on the frame — but embedded in the middle of the mesh body. A similar version has four more set in the same way. Both of these jewel inset purses are adorned with long fancy faux gemstone carry chains.

These types of purses were a contrast to the predominantly floral, rug motif, and figural designs of the Mandalian Company. Whiting and Davis raised customers' awareness to their products through strong advertising campaigns that boosted sales tremendously. But quality not quantity was the Mandalian goal. Consequently, not many advertisements by Mandalian are found today. Purses by this company were of high production standards that often took longer to produce than those of their rival, the Whiting and Davis Company.

By 1944, the Mandalian Manufacturing Company was sold to its competitor, Charles Whiting. All patent rights and holdings were included in the sale, necessary because of a lack of funds and scarcity of metals due to the production of war materials. Mandalian died five years later, on June 6, 1949, at the age of 80.

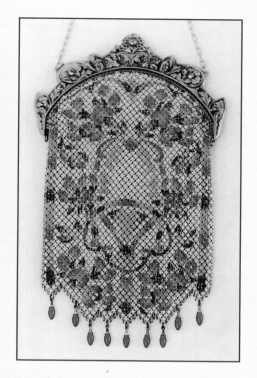

Mandalian enameled mesh purse with fancy arched frame and teardrop enameled fringe. 5 x 8. Author's collection. $800.00 – 1,000.00.

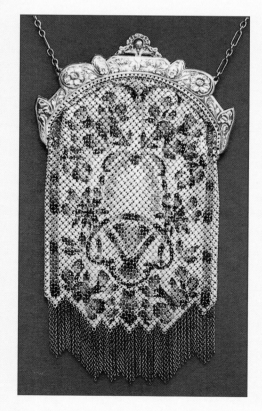

The identical pattern with many variations: color of enamel, fringe type, and frame color. It is interesting to see how the purse appearance changes with these different details. 5 x 8 From the collection of Elaine Lehn. $800.00 – 1,000.00.

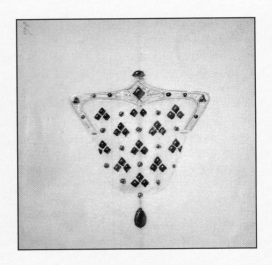

Edgerton Ames Bliss as a boy in 1854, and 50 years later (1904) as the proud owner of the E.A. Bliss Company. Courtesy of the Napier Company archives.

A design for a small jeweled mesh purse for the E.A. Bliss Company. Courtesy of the Napier Company archives.

Lovely jeweled frame mesh purse by the E.A. Bliss Company. It has ball drops and measures 6 x 6. The Curiosity Shop. $395.00 – 495.00.

This became the location that housed the E.A. Bliss Company. Taken from a sketch made by C. Robert Fasey, this was formerly the Old Flint Glassworks Company. Courtesy of the Napier Company archives.

In the 1920s, the Bliss Company became the Napier Company when James H. Napier was elected president. Courtesy of the Napier Company archives.

Surrealistic flowers adorn this sassy Mandalian purse. Deeply embossed silvertone frame. 4½ x 9. Author's collection. $800.00 – 1,000.00.

In 1921, Napier/Bliss introduced "The DuBarry" vanity purse. *The Jeweler's Circular.*

A Whiting and Davis Dresden-style purse with embossed gold frame. 5 x 6. From the collection of Paula Higgins. $395.00 – 495.00.

Mandalian peach colored heart motif enameled purse with teal teardrops and a mint green background color. 4 x 9. Author's collection. $1,000.00+.

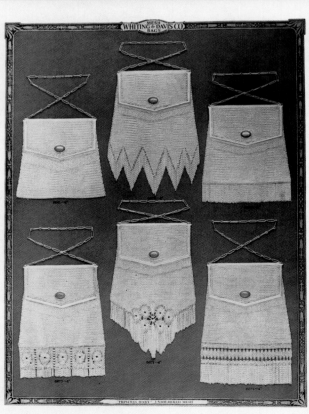

The Princess Mary fine ring mesh purse by the Whiting and Davis Company, 1922. Whiting & Davis Catalog, photograph by Walter Kitik.

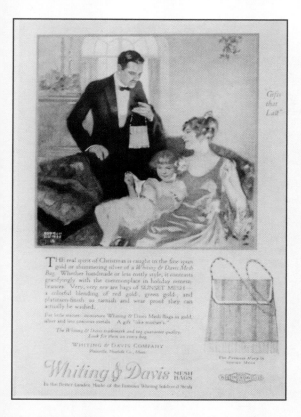

The Princess Mary in sunset mesh is featured in this Christmas season advertisement by Whiting and Davis.

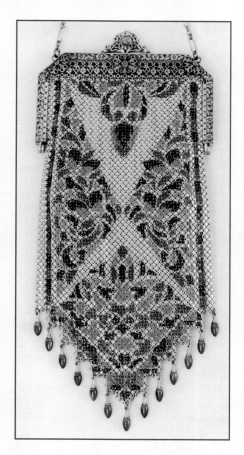

A filigree frame sets off the colorful envelope pattern Mandalian purse. Accented by teal teardrops, this purse has a silk lining. 4 x 9. Author's collection. $800.00 – 1,000.00.

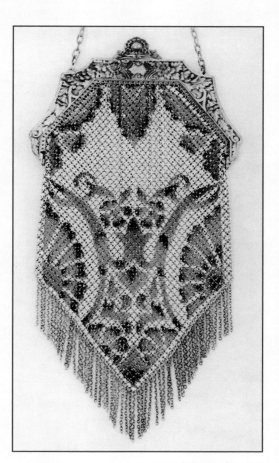

A Mandalian purse in a striking enamel color combination including orange and mint green, creating an almost fan-like motif. 5 x 9. The Curiosity Shop. $600.00 – 800.00.

Tiny (baby) mesh enameled purse with a lovely looped chain fringe and delicately enameled frame. 4½ x 10½. The Curiosity Shop. $800.00 – 1,000.00.

Mesh purses were made of a variety of materials including gunmetal, silver, composition metal, and German silver, to name a few.

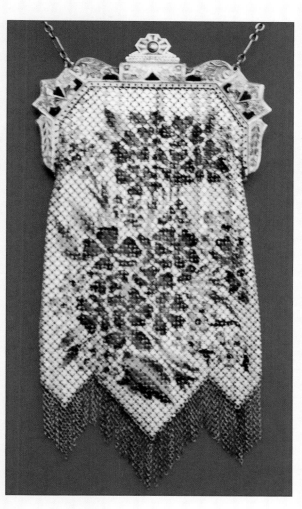

Floral enameled mesh Mandalian with three pointed fringe. Elaborate openworked enameled frame. 5 x 9. From the collection of Elaine Lehn. $650.00 – 850.00.

The main American plant of the Whiting and Davis Company in Plainville, Massachusetts. Courtesy of the Napier Company archives.

A pretty confetti colored frame matches the silk-screen body on this mesh purse by Whiting and Davis. 5 x 6. From the collection of Paula Higgins. $295.00 – 395.00.

Shown open, the silk lining has a floral motif pattern to match the body of the bag. From the collection of Paula Higgins.

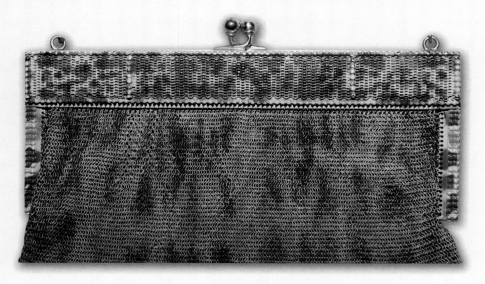

A close-up of the matching colored frame reveals attention to detail.

Poinsettia motif floral purse by Mandalian. The teardrops have lost some enamel; still, an unusual purse. 5 x 8½. The Curiosity Shop. $695.00 – 895.00 if perfect.

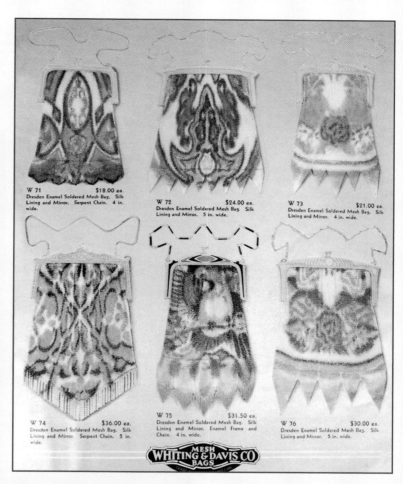

W 71	$18.00 ea.
Dresden Enamel Soldered Mesh Bag. Silk Lining and Mirror. Serpent Chain. 4 in. wide.	

W 72	$24.00 ea.
Dresden Enamel Soldered Mesh Bag. Silk Lining and Mirror. 5 in. wide.	

W 73	$21.00 ea.
Dresden Enamel Soldered Mesh Bag. Silk Lining and Mirror. 4 in. wide.	

W 74	$36.00 ea.
Dresden Enamel Soldered Mesh Bag. Silk Lining and Mirror. Serpent Chain. 5 in. wide.	

W 75	$31.50 ea.
Dresden Enamel Soldered Mesh Bag. Silk Lining and Mirror. Enamel Frame and Chain. 4 in. wide.	

W 76	$30.00 ea.
Dresden Enamel Soldered Mesh Bag. Silk Lining and Mirror. 5 in. wide.	

WHITING & DAVIS CO. MESH BAGS

Colorful Dresden mesh purses as advertised by the Whiting and Davis Company. *The Jeweler's Circular*, 1931.

A Whiting and Davis retail advertisement for a "Spanish lace on polished gold" enameled mesh bag. This purse is described as having "petit armor mesh," otherwise known as baby flat mesh. *The Jeweler's Circular*, December 1929.

THE NEW SPANISH MODE IN SHEER GOLD AND LACY BLACK~

NATIONALLY ADVERTISED for CHRISTMAS DISPLAYS

"No Interesting Woman ever has too many Costume Bags," said Paul Poiret when he was asked to name the sort of gift most sure to please.

And no retailer of Whiting & Davis creations ever lacks for new, nationally advertised and temptingly beautiful Costume Bags to win more holiday sales. Display them now. Let this new model —Spanish lace on polished gold—mark your Christmas displays with that air of smart originality which is your store's sign of leadership as well as ours. By its authentic quality of style and craftsmanship, a nationally advertised Whiting & Davis Costume Bag in your window-display invites the public to visit all departments.

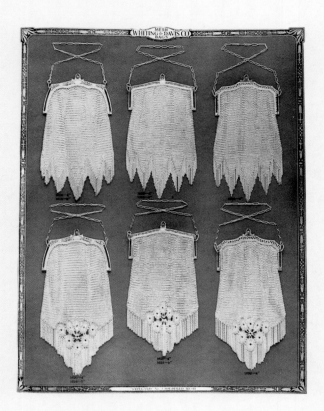

Whiting and Davis fine ring mesh purses featuring fancy Venetian fringe. Whiting & Davis Catalog, 1922, photograph by Walter Kitik.

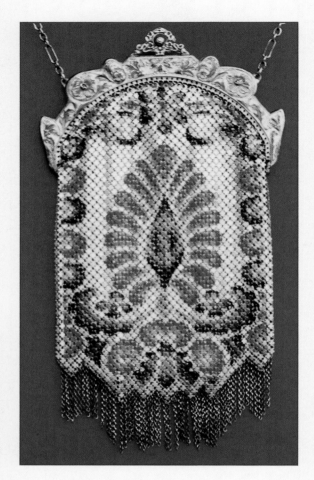

Mandalian enameled mesh purse with arched enameled frame. Bold central design, seven pointed fringe. 5 x 9. From the collection of Elaine Lehn. $800.00 – 1,000.00.

1920s fine mesh purse with intricate fringe on the sides. A celluloid pink and blue floral, bell-shaped pull covers the loops through which the foxtail chain is threaded, enabling the bag to close. The inner hoop circle creates the form of the purse. Finished with the original mesh tassel. Unmarked, but probably by the Whiting and Davis Company. 3¼ x 8. From the collection of Paula Higgins. $495.00 – 595.00.

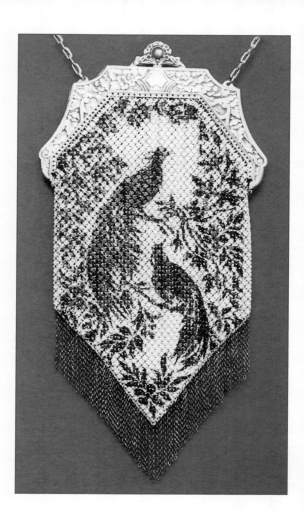

Mandalian enameled mesh featuring a beautiful pair of peacocks. Silvertone frame, chain fringe. 4½ x 8. From the collection of Elaine Lehn. $695.00 – 895.00.

Another version of the Mandalian enameled mesh peacock, this one with three pointed fringe and multicolored body. 3½ x 8. The Curiosity Shop. $695.00 – 895.00.

An unusual peacock motif unmarked purse. 5 x 7. The Curiosity Shop. $695.00 – 895.00.

Two lovely peacock Mandalian purses. This clearly shows the difference when varying colored enamels are used, despite the obvious fringe loss on one. Each measures 3½ x 7. The Curiosity Shop. $695.00 – 895.00 each if perfect.

Another variance in the Mandalian peacock purse, ending in a fancy double teardrop as well as chain fringe. 3½ x 7. The Curiosity Shop. $695.00 – 895.00.

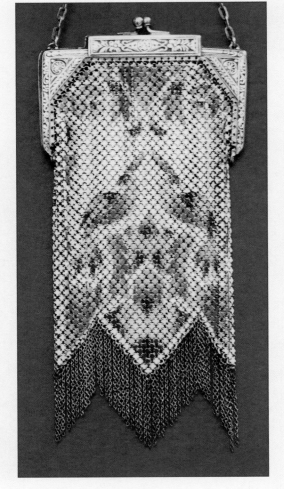

Mandalian enameled mesh Bird of Paradise motif purse with fringe. 4 x 7. From the collection of Elaine Lehn. $675.00 – 895.00.

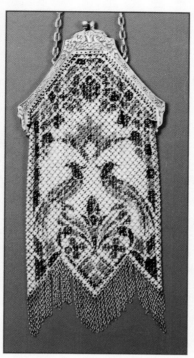

Facing peacock motif by Mandalian. This originally sold for $4.00. 3½ x 7. The Curiosity Shop. $650.00 – 850.00.

Birds decorate this plainly framed Mandalian. 5 x 7. From the collection of Elaine Lehn. $650.00 – 850.00.

Whiting and Davis enameled mesh purse with cockatoo motif. Delicately embossed frame. 4½ x 7. The Curiosity Shop. $695.00 – 895.00.

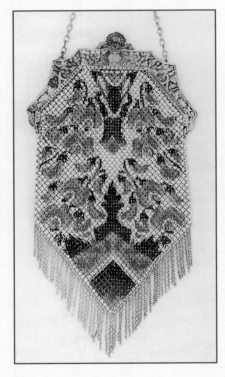

Charming Mandalian purse with a floral design resembling orchids or "ladies' slippers." Deeply embossed frame in silvertone. 4½ x 8. Author's collection. $750.00 – 1,000.00.

Swans glide gracefully across a quiet lake on this Mandalian. 4½ x 7. From the collection of Elaine Lehn. $1,000.00+.

1920s fine mesh purse by Whiting and Davis Company, finished with a tassel. Central adjustable carry strap. 3½ x 9. The Curiosity Shop. $375.00 – 495.00.

Catalog page from Whiting and Davis Mesh Bags, 1922. Courtesy of the Napier Company, photograph by Walter Kitik.

Mandalian enameled mesh purse with filigree frame. Multi-floral design. 4½ x 8. The Curiosity Shop. $500.00 – 700.00.

An enameled frame and teardrops were manufactured to fit perfectly with this lovely Mandalian purse. 4 x 9. From the collection of Elaine Lehn. $600.00 – 800.00.

By the Mandalian Manufacturing Company, this Martha Washington purse was designed to emulate the brown satin ribbon-worked, embroidered reticule that the famous first lady not only made and but also carried during George Washington's 1789 inauguration. 3½ x 10. From the collection of Elaine Lehn. $225.00 – 325.00.

Martha Washington's dress and purse are depicted in this photograph from The Smithsonian Institute.

All dressed up and ready to venture out on a cold winter day, a lady must remember her mesh purse!

Just before World War II, Whiting and Davis introduced a new style of mesh bag called Alu-mesh. It was a white summer bag with large mesh links that sold in the price range of $4.95 to $7.95. 7 x 8. The Curiosity Shop, photograph by Irene Clarke. $25.00 – 75.00.

The Alu-mesh purse by Whiting and Davis was available with many different frame styles. 7 x 8. The Curiosity Shop. $25.00 – 75.00.

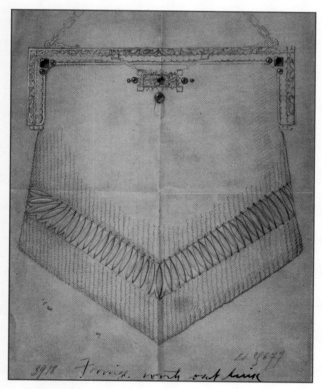

An original French design drawing of an unusual jeweled mesh purse created for the Bliss Company, executed on a special wax paper that was tipped in color. Courtesy of the Napier Company archives.

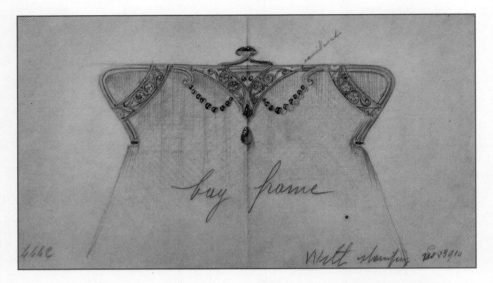

Dated April of 1912, this original design drawing by the Bliss Company features an elaborate jeweled frame and blue stone pendant drop. Courtesy of the Napier Company archives.

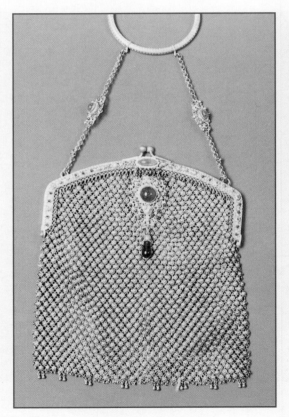

Rare and unusual unmarked heavy mesh purse with a jeweled frame, carry chain, and pendant drop. This type of purse was made prior to the production of colored mesh purses. Notice the curious shaped metal links, much different than the familiar ones by the Mandalian Manufacturing or the Whiting and Davis Company. A generous 7 x 8½ . Author's collection. Rare.

An unmarked goldtone gate-top mesh purse, this frame is also known as an "accordion top" because of the ability of the frame's neck to be expanded to access the interior of the purse much like the mechanics of the musical instrument. A jeweled lid snaps on atop the purse when the neck is pulled close. The carry chain is attached to a chatelaine style hook. 2 x 3¾. The Curiosity Shop. $75.00 – 95.00.

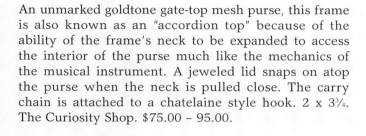

Set to dangle from a chatelaine, wrist, or pinkie, the mesh purse helped to make a lady a regal sight.

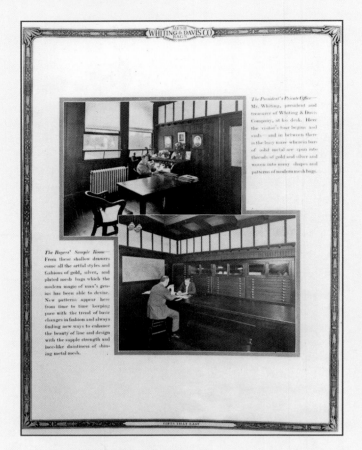

The buyer's sample room in the Whiting and Davis Company. Kept in shallow drawers, the newest styles, patterns, and colors of mesh bags were waiting to be shown to prospective clients. Courtesy of the Napier Company archives.

Whiting and Davis purses with a wide flared skirt originally ranged in price from about $15.00 to $18.00. The level of expertise and the amount of material used to manufacture these were greater than the average sized bags. Bold geometric design with gilded openworked frame. 8 x 9. The Curiosity Shop. $350.00 – 475.00.

A 1924 advertisement for a Whiting and Davis "utility mesh bag." This purse is described as being silk lined with a vanity mirror and as a perfect complement to the powder compact purse, the Delysia shown on the ladies' arm. *The Delineator.*

An example of a Whiting and Davis beadlite floral motif purse. This type of metal link was used to emulate tiny glass beads as opposed to the flat mesh style often used. With an Art Deco style silvertone frame and a snake carry chain, this purse also has the unusual wide flared skirt. 6½ x 7. The Curiosity Shop. $295.00 – 375.00.

With the same floral pattern and beadlite mesh links, this purse has a variance in the body color and frame style/color. Whiting and Davis, 5 x 8. The Curiosity Shop. $295.00 – 375.00.

Skilled artisans with delicate tools soldered joints and ball knobs onto purse frames in the assembly room at the Whiting and Davis Company. Courtesy of the Napier Company archives.

Butterfly figural enameled mesh purse by Mandalian. A lovely twin Art Nouveau style design. 3½ x 7. The Curiosity Shop. $450.00 – 595.00.

In mint green and purple, this unearthly, beautiful butterfly is the focal point of this Mandalian. This originally sold for $4.00. 4 x 7. The Curiosity Shop. $495.00 – 595.00.

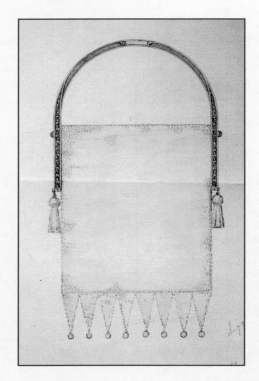

Tipped in color, this elaborate rigid handled and multi-tasseled mesh purse design is by the Bliss Company from the early twentieth century. Courtesy of the Napier Company archives.

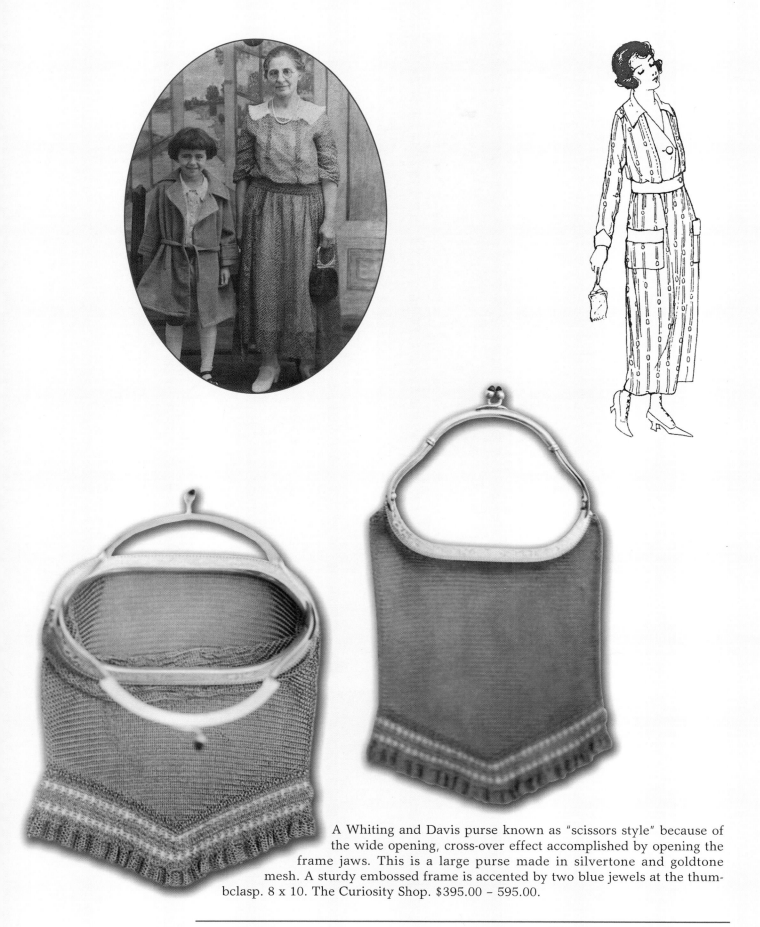

A Whiting and Davis purse known as "scissors style" because of the wide opening, cross-over effect accomplished by opening the frame jaws. This is a large purse made in silvertone and goldtone mesh. A sturdy embossed frame is accented by two blue jewels at the thumbclasp. 8 x 10. The Curiosity Shop. $395.00 – 595.00.

Rare figural Mandalian featuring a woodland scene with a graceful leaping deer. 4½ x 8. Author's collection. Rare.

An extremely rare figural by Whiting and Davis featuring elephants performing at a circus. Colorful baby mesh is utilized. The interior is lined. Attached to the gilt frame is a snake style carry chain. 4 x 6½. The Curiosity Shop. Very rare.

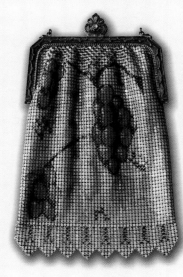

In baby flat mesh, a rare scenic Whiting and Davis depicting grape clusters. This originally sold for $18.00 in 1927 and was advertised as being constructed of "extra fine weave." 4 x 6½. Author's collection. Rare.

This group of scenic Mandalians demonstrates subtle differences using the same subject matter while varying the color scheme. Notice how the use of a goldtone fringe and frame compare with those manufactured with matching silvertone frame and fringe. Some collectors like to find purses with all the color variances. 3½ x 7. The Curiosity Shop. $700.00 – 900.00 each.

Yet another Mandalian with a vase and floral pattern utilizing a different color scheme. 3½ x 7. The Curiosity Shop. $700.00 – 900.00.

This large Whiting and Davis purse has a detailed figural/scenic motif. A couple lounges on the grass in the foreground against a castle scenic background. Vandyke fringe. 8 x 11. The Curiosity Shop. Rare.

A lined Whiting and Davis purse featuring a castle in the distance and several seagulls floating overhead. Black enameled frame. 4 x 6. The Curiosity Shop. $600.00 – 800.00.

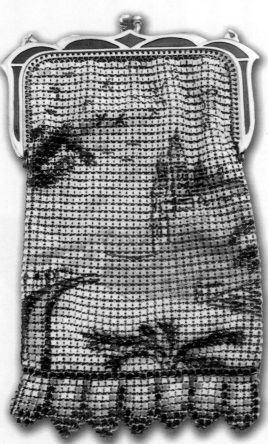

A Mandalian with an unusual pattern, drops. 4 x 6½. The Curiosity Shop. $495.00 – 695.00.

Mandalian enameled mesh with drops and a frame that is sometimes referred to as "stained glass" because of metal pockets that hold enamel. 5 x 9. The Curiosity Shop. $700.00 – 900.00.

Unmarked ring mesh purse. 4 x 5. The Curiosity Shop.
$75.00 – 155.00.

Dated September 18, 1911, an original mesh purse design by
the Bliss Company prior to the Napier Company name change.
Courtesy of the Napier Company archives.

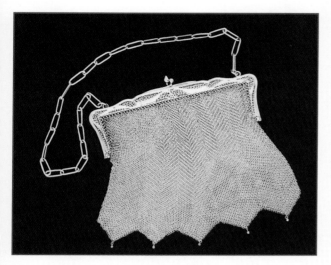
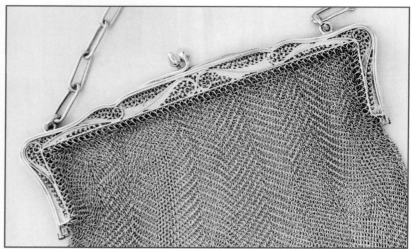

Heavy unmarked purse with a filigree frame, a unique ring mesh pattern, finished with tiny drops. 6 x 7. The Curiosity Shop, photograph by Irene Clarke. $75.00 – 150.00.

The Gloria Bag by Mandalian Manufacturing Company. These purses have a unique jointed frame referred to as "bracelet style." This one has a touch of enameling on the frame, a subtle Art Nouveau pattern, and fringe stemming from several points, the combination of which make it very desirable. 4¼ x 7. From the collection of Elaine Lehn. Rare.

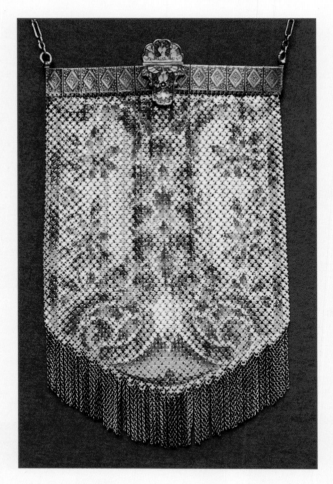

A Gloria Bag by Mandalian with a lightly enameled closure clasp. An almost random floral pattern decorates this unique purse. 4¼ x 7. From the collection of Elaine Lehn. Rare.

A popular floral pattern for the Mandalian Gloria Bag. Shown open, the "bracelet style" frame is quite evident. This purse finishes in a chain fringe that frames the rounded body at the bottom. 4¼ x 7. The Curiosity Shop. Rare.

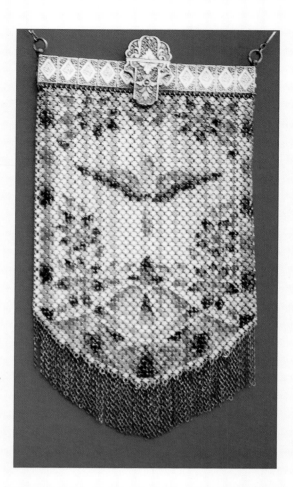

Mandalian Gloria Bag. From the collection of Elaine Lehn. Rare.

Original design drawing for a purse of "ring mesh with inside metal wire at the bottom." Courtesy of the Napier Company archives.

Sterling ring mesh purse with fancy eagle motif frame. 2½ x 3. The Curiosity Shop, photograph by Irene Clarke. $95.00 – 175.00.

French mesh purse designed with bezel set rhinestones and an arched frame set with tiny faux pearls; made during the Art Deco period. 5 x 6. The Curiosity Shop. $275.00 – 475.00.

Designed in the early twentieth century, this ring mesh purse was intended to have a metal wire inside and a purse frame with stamping. Courtesy of the Napier Company archives.

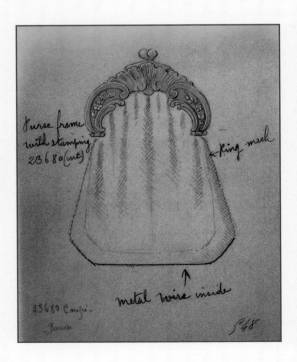

Unsigned, but probably by the Whiting and Davis Company. This ring mesh purse has drops along the sides and a metal bell shaped pull top and a mesh tassel. 3¼ x 8. The Curiosity Shop. $495.00 – 595.00.

Rare esoteric jewel inset enameled mesh purse by Whiting and Davis. Fancy bezel set jeweled carry chain. The large stone appears on both sides. Author's collection. Very rare.

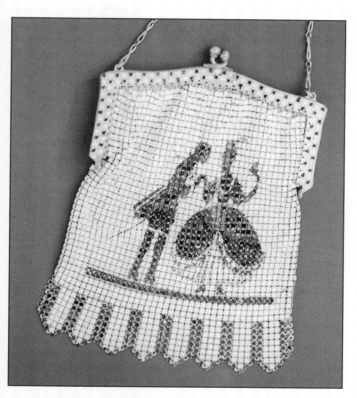

Black enameled silhouetted figures of a lady and her beau are featured on a Whiting and Davis mesh purse. Enameled checkerboard frame, linked carry chain. 5½ x 7. Author's collection. Rare.

In the early Middle Ages, while knights were fighting far from home, their ladies spent many days cross-stitching embroidery. The fabrics they made from rough cross-stitch or half cross-stitch gave the castle of the Middle Ages a warm and comfortable atmosphere. In fact, hand embroidery is one of the oldest arts, spanning many centuries. Handwork was generally accomplished on very coarse materials. Much later, the number of stitches on the same area increased and the work became finer.

The art of hand embroidery underwent changes in the rococo period when the smallest articles of daily use were bestowed with more charm and appeal. The desire for luxurious housing decors in even the smallest of rooms resulted in the art of fine embroidery. And so the shift from the coarse, half-cross embroidery to small point embroidery, also called petit point, ensued. To the naked eye it appears as a mosaic of small points. Both the opulent style of the rococo period and the art of fine petit point stitching were later instrumental in the making of fabric purses.

The likeness of Madame de Pompadour (1721 – 1764) is depicted on lovely, turn of the twentieth century petit point purses. Although these vintage purses were obviously made many years after her death, they are a testament to the fact that she was fondly remembered for an expanse of time. Not only was she a beautiful, cultivated woman and the official mistress of King Louis XV, she was also an icon of court culture. Her place in high society during the French Enlightenment period is recorded through the many wonderful portraits by outstanding artists, and has been immortalized in painstaking stitches on charming purses.

Great prosperity during Louis XV's reign (1723 – 1774) encouraged a zest for elegance and a substantial flair for luxury. The combination of Madame de Pompadour's immense popularity, exquisite taste, and unbridled wealth greatly influenced fashion in France.

Charming petit point with a figural scene of Madame de Pompadour carrying a basket laden with flowers. Duplicated from a portrait, all of the important fine points found in the painting, from the neatly tied bows under her chin and on her shoulder, to the multi-strand pearl bracelet, are present on the purse. The sterling frame, generously embossed with flowers and roses, matches the elaborate rococo décor around the central figural medallion. The reverse depicts a lovely vase spilling over with flowers. Perhaps the flowers Madame gathered? 7½ x 8. From the collection of Diane Goldfarb. Rare.

Using copies of historic portraits as guidance, it was less difficult for petit point artists to accurately duplicate Pompadour's likeness and reproduce it, with their own variations, in the form of carefully stitched purses. In fact, the purse that portrays Pompadour holding a flower, her arm through a basket laden with flowers, was most assuredly duplicated from a specific portrait. The important fine points found in the painting, from the neatly tied bows both under her chin and on her shoulder, to the multi-strand pearl bracelet, are present on the purse. The only difference is that she faces the opposite direction.

A generous woman, she encouraged such fine painters as Francois Boucher, whom she sat for, sculptors such as Jean-Baptiste Pigalle and writers like Voltaire while commissioning images of herself that would enhance her status at court. With the help of these many portraits and through the purses later made from them, the fashions of her lifetime and her delicate, refined femininity have been fastidiously recorded.

As mistress of the house, she promoted the decorative arts, securing the king's interest in the manufacture of porcelain at Sevres, where it was produced. She keenly entertained the restless king by organizing festivals, overseeing shows, planning dinner parties and other activities, as well as stimulating his interest in architecture and gardening.

The décor of her many town and country residences were finished in a delicate floral rococo

manner referred to as "Pompadour style." Both purses' depictions of Madame de Pompadour in a central medallion, encompassed by lovely floral decoration, were the petit point artist's way of immortalizing her, permanently encircling her with the rococo style that she loved and surrounded herself with in life.

The ladies of the Viennese court, under the great Empress Maria Theresia (1717 – 1780), completed many beautiful tapestries that were found in the court museums and castles of that period. The

This depiction of Madame de Pompadour in a central medallion encompassed by a plethora of delicate flowers, was the petit point artist's way of immortalizing her, permanently encircling her with the Rococo style that she loved and surrounded herself with in life. A lovely color combination against the blue and gold background, crowned with a carnelian jeweled cast frame. 7½ x 8. From the collection of Diane Goldfarb. Rare.

love for this particular art form found its way amongst the people. A natural talent for combining beautiful colors enabled them to discover new possibilities, and the expertise in that field has been handed down from generation to generation.

While designs changed, techniques remained the same, although the stitch itself became finer. This advancement in petit point embroidery brought about the demand for decorative items which resulted in handbags, powder compacts, and many small objets d'art.

Needlepoint embroidery has up to four points per centimeter, which translates to 16 points per square centimeter or 103 points per square inch. This method is used in the production of wall decorations and floor carpets, chair, seat, and footstool covers, as well as afternoon and shopping purses.

Petit point embroidery has anywhere from 6 to 22 points per centimeter and 36 to 484 points per square centimeter, translating to 232 to 3,122 points per square inch, and is used for evening bags, powder compacts, cigarette cases, and many other articles. The finest and most delicate of these embroideries was accomplished with the aid of a magnifying glass to enable the extremely fine needle to be inserted through the web-like silk canvas used as a base. The delicate embroidery, the beauty of the design, and the harmony of the colors combine to become a masterpiece.

To enhance the beauty of a purse, details like gussets, might be elaborate with tiny stitched roses, or have a carefully applied design of metallic gold thread. This oftentimes decorative and complimentary, yet necessary, insert in a seam provides for expansion and reinforcement. It is found along the bottom of the purse, usually continuing up to the frame joints or drawstring top (in the case of a reticule purse). An artistic gusset is one example of how antique purse makers would transform a necessary part of a purse into a miniature work of art.

One thing is certain: whether it is a framed purse or reticule, there was a tremendous amount of work involved in the production of a vintage petit point bag or a quality tapestry purse, from the gusset to the selection of the frame or header and drawstring material.

During the nineteenth century in the United States, learning and practicing various forms of needlework

French embroidered reticule of silk taffeta worked in polychrome silk and metallic threads with a rococo floral design in satin stitches. Trimmed with a wide metallic gusset and decorated with a yellow silk ribbon drawstring. The purse, in an ornate, highly stylized design typical of the eighteenth century, is shown with a miniature of Madame de Pompadour. 5½ x 4½. From the collection of Paula Higgins. $550.00 – 750.00.

Extremely fine stitched petit point purse in rich colors depicting lovers in a pastoral scene. The cherub happily watches the couple from above as he swings from the pendant drop which dangles from the semi precious jeweled frame. The reverse shows a different scene typical of high quality petit points. 6½ x 8. From the collection of Paula Jay Wolslager. Rare.

Petit point figural purse with the same scene. These pastoral scenes featuring lambs and lovers were popular among artists. High quality purse frames sometimes contain a genuine cameo, as is the case here. 6½ x 8. From the collection of Diane Goldfarb. $750.00 – 950.00.

the 1920s. A popular whimsical item for Americans, these bags were colorful and often had solid jade or glass bracelet rings instead of carry chains. Ladies' magazines advertised these imported purses which helped to create demand.

Vintage purses were also imported from Turkey. Machine embroidered on gauze with fancy gold metal covered thread, they could contain an early "artificial silk" lining (a term used for early synthetics from about 1890 to 1920). Even then, these Turkish bags revitalized old styles that were used for years in the export business. These purses have an appeal all their own, but should not be confused with their much earlier counterparts which the Turks sought to emulate.

Scandinavian exporters were another source offering purses. Their popular wool chatelaine purses contained Norwegian wool embroidery called Rosesaum, a term for rose work. They also included a hook on the frame for attachment along the waist. The purses were nicely made with attention to detail although it should be noted that wool

Of Scandinavian (Norway) origin, this turn of the twentieth century wool chatelaine with Norwegian wool embroidery is called Rosesaum (rose work). This purse may have been part of a folk dress outfit or national costume. 8 x 12. From the collection of Paula Higgins. $250.00 – 350.00.

became popular and fashionable for young women. Generally, during this time, homemakers did not work outside the home unless lured by pay incentives from work in mills or factories. In the Victorian era, women embroidered purses, napkins, handkerchiefs, chair seats, pillows, compact cases, and a variety of other items during leisure time. Lovely needlework, petit point, and satin stitched purses were made both as a hobby and for their practical enjoyment.

Two classes of purse embroideries are flat (art) embroidery and decorative (raised novelty) embroidery. Flat embroidery includes all ornamental needlework including tapestry, crewel, wool, silk, linen, cotton, metallic, or gold threads that are applied directly to the fabric of the purse. Embroideries wrought of chenille are called raised novelty embroidery.

Stitching open space in a canvas between the warp and weft threads, using a threaded needle to place stitches across from one opening to the next in a diagonal direction is called needlepoint. Fine work of this type in stitches half the sizes of the needlepoint stitches are called petit point. An even tinier stitch is called micropoint. This type of stitch can make a needlework piece look so fine that it appears to be a tapestry at first glance. The term for larger stitches, nearing twice the area of the needlepoint stitch, is gross point.

Chinese embroidery purses made from silk were imported between the turn of the century and

A naughty motif figural petit point stitched purse. The front side depicts the gentleman with his hat in his hand and flowers behind his back as she looks away. The reverse is a scene of the garden, now empty, her pink dress resting on a vacant tree bench with a mute statue as the sole witness. 7 x 7. Author's collection. Rare.

was rarely used in fine needlework due to its coarse nature. These charming Scandinavian purses may have been part of folk dress outfits or national costumes.

In Scotland, fine glass beaded envelope purses were embroidered with gold metal paillettes. These glistening clusters provided a decorative trim on the purse fabric. Bound in silk and metal threads, they were typical of the eighteenth century.

A myriad of needlework employed in purse making was in use over periods of many years. Tapestry stitch is an example of a stitch commonly used in embroidery and in Berlin work. It is raised from the canvas by virtue of being worked over two horizontal threads. Tambour work was also widely used. It is made with a fine chain stitch accomplished with a hook.

A satin stitch, generally used in old French embroidery on silk and flannel, is made by passing a thread from one outline of the design to the other, back and forth, leaving an equal amount of material on both sides of the work. These patterns were run through with filling stitches, leaving the work, when finished, with a slightly raised, rounded effect.

People often made handcrafted purses during earlier times. Some of these homespun bags utilized a variety of materials and techniques and were quite well made. For instance, in the early

twentieth century, moiré was used, giving the fabric sheen while providing an irregular wavy finish. For the lining, sarcenet, a soft thin silk in plain weave, might have been used. Beading and other decorative accessories could then be added to give the purse a look all its own.

Painted "Theorem" purses were made with stencils for color, usually on velvet. Cording may have outlined the purse and accent tassels were of silk and chenille. After being colored, the paint was then set with a type of gum mixture. For a purse to be highly desirable both sides should have a different scene and it must be artistically well executed.

Some homemade purses from earlier times were fashioned with recycled materials. One example transformed a piece of stiff writing paper or cardboard backing, reusing it to provide a hidden structure for a flap over purse.

Another type of handmade purse contained the maker's name or initials. In late eighteenth century America, one such purse had the needle worker's name, "Amanda T. Guerig" worked into the design. Typical for the time period, a "v" was used for a "u." The middle initial is a "t," not an "f." It was achieved using queen stitch embroidery — the most difficult embroidery stitch. The geometric strawberry design was also typical of the time period.

The process for creating professionally made petit point bags began in painter's studios in the early twentieth century. One can imagine the creative inspiration of these purses while studying their designs. Here, the artistic spirit is embodied in the fascinating arrangements the artist renders first in an original charcoal design, using the Dutch Masters and romantic artists for motivation. Other

Refreshingly different, because of its heart shaped jeweled frame, this petit point purse has tiny faux pearls decorating its entire length. A figure is apparent in the medallion portion of the purse. 7 x 7. The Curiosity Shop. $500.00 – 700.00.

Figural tapestry purse, elaborate embossed gilt frame with a plunger top. A simple black gusset trims the bottom. 6 x 8. From the collection of Diane Goldfarb. $750.00 – 950.00.

---

inspirations included floral arrangements and still-lifes, which were the original creations of artisans in the studios. Pastoral scenes featuring lovers and lambs were also quite popular.

If a charcoal sketch was a success, a watercolor painting was made from it. Should the color scheme prove satisfactory, the watercolor was transferred into rubrics, onto millimeter graph paper appearing mosaic-like, with each small square having a separate color.

This type of work required enormous experience and skill. Used for the actual pattern of the embroidery, it was called the "point" by the artists. The completion of such a point could take weeks and, by itself, was considered an achievement even before the rest of the process was completed.

The point was passed to a studio assistant whose task was to select various embroidery yarns required for a particular piece. More than 500 color shades were often required to produce one quality petit point purse. Only experienced workers with a strong sense of color, design, and imagination were able to render this selection for the creation of the embroidery. It took a surprising amount of training and expertise.

Once the charcoal was drawn, a watercolor was made, and the yarn was selected, then the enormous task of petit point embroidery began. The silk gauze used in rough point work (a strong cotton weave) was put into the embroidery frame. The embroidery pattern was then positioned in front of the worker as the color point from the pattern was counted and then embroidered onto the gauze. One half cross-stitch after another appeared, and the petit point design slowly took shape.

For each painted square on the pattern, two stitches on the silk gauze were needed, giving the appearance of a point on the surface. The first stitch was started on the left side of the material and was worked upward, while the second one was worked from the top downward. In order to keep to the design, the color of the yarn had to be changed constantly in the needle.

Depending on the delicacy of the work, there might be from 72 to 968 stitches per square centimeter, so that there are 36 to 484, or half as many, points on the surface. As soon as the embroidery was ready (this may have taken up to twenty-four weeks of steady work), the wooden embroidery frame was taken away and the work was carefully checked with a magnifying glass to assure that not a single stitch was missed. Tapestries were made in the same way except that instead of silk gauze, a stronger cotton weave, called Stramin or canvas, was used.

The embroidery on cotton weave was coarser and not always suitable where the design included figures. In this case, the thread of the cotton weave was split, making it possible to double the number of stitches on the running centimeter or accomplish four times the number on the square centimeter. Consequently, a purse very often shows two different grades of embroidery.

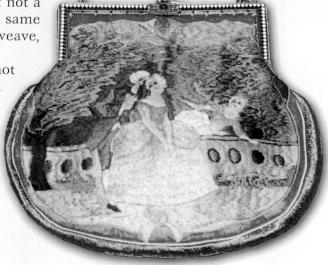

Silk stitched multi-figural purse with a jeweled frame. This type of silk stitched figural purse with a romantic theme is a favorite among collectors. 6 x 7. From the collection of Diane Goldfarb. $850.00+.

As soon as the embroidery for an evening bag was ready, a purse frame was designed and produced by jewelers. Functional, yet aesthetic, it was chosen according to the value of the embroidery. If it was marked trinity plate, it consisted of metal treated with copper, silver, and nickel plating. High quality embroidery and petit point purses might have a fancy frame that contains genuine cameos or semi-precious stones.

Many artists and experienced workers were engaged to design embroidery patterns or assist with various other stages to complete these works of art. Years of experience and creative abilities were essential to the success of the work: the practical, timeless, and fashionable petit point purse.

A lovely Aubusson tapestry purse featuring hidden Cupids peering at lovers. Notice the scallop shaped jeweled purse frame. 6 x 9. From the collection of Diane Goldfarb. Rare.

A finely stitched petit point insert of a lone musician surrounded by brown crocheted and bronze colored beads. Twisted loop fringe, simple arched frame. 6 x 9½. From the collection of Diane Goldfarb. Rare.

A circa 1910 – 1920 fine petit point figural scenic purse with a different scene on the reverse. Unusual enameled frame. 6½ x 8½. From the collection of Paula Higgins. $700.00 – 900.00.

Extraordinary Austrian tiny silk stitched figural purse. Silver frame set with a genuine ruby. 6 x 7. Author's collection. Very rare.

Close-ups reveal attention to detail.

Reverse depicts a medallion emblem within a border of ornately placed pearls.

Tapestry purse with a unique pastoral theme. The gentleman offers the lady a blue bird in a cage while his dog looks on. With a plunger top and detailed frame. French, turn of the twentieth century. 8 x 9. From the collection of Diane Goldfarb. $850.00 – 1,000.00.

Beautiful tambour worked embroidered purse on silk moiré executed in a light, flowing flower, ribbon, and bows design. Fine handmade lacework with a silk drawstring and lining. This lovely piece may have been used for sewing articles and is also known as a knotting bag or sewing purse. The work is typical of the last quarter of the eighteenth century. 8½ x 11½. From the collection of Paula Higgins. $1,200.00 + .

A charming and colorful petit point purse with a barefoot lady as the focal point. On the reverse, two ladies lounge amidst pastoral surroundings. Jeweled and enameled frame. 8 x 9. From the collection of Diane Goldfarb. $950.00 – 1,200.00.

Notice the elaborate rose and floral gusset along the bottom of the purse. An artistic gusset is one example of how purse makers transformed a functional portion of the purse to create a miniature work of art.

Swings were popular subjects for vintage purses. Shown here on this petit point purse, lovers enjoy a gentle ride on an oversized swing. A vase spills over with roses to form the elaborate frame design. The reverse shows a pointed rooftop pavilion. 6 x 9. The Curiosity Shop. $650.00 – 795.00.

Scenic petit point purse with delicate marcasite frame. 7 x 7. The Curiosity Shop. $495.00 – 650.00.

This needlework purse with a jeweled frame re-creates Jean-Honoré Fragonard's famous painting, *The Swing*. The Baron de Saint-Julien commissioned the artwork. 6 x 9. The Curiosity Shop. $595.00 – 795.00.

Artists at work — a painter's studio where patterns for embroidered purses were made.

A lovely needlework flower basket motif purse with a jeweled frame. The stitching here is not as finely executed as with a petit point. The Curiosity Shop. $300.00 – 475.00.

Petit point figurals with lovers and lambs were popular. In some cases, over 500 silk color variations were used to make a single purse. Here, a genuine cameo embellishes the jeweled frame. 8 x 8. Author's collection. Rare.

Elaborate tapestry purse with black enameled frame. 7 x 9. The Curiosity Shop. $450.00 – 550.00.

A floral purse in needlepoint with a simple enameled and lightly jeweled frame. 6 x 7. The Curiosity Shop. $295.00 – 395.00.

Securely attaching a needlework purse to its frame is a final stage of assembly.

A combination of petit point and needle-point stitches decorates this unique purse. The central figures are executed in fine petit point, yet the floral rococo style border is finished with a larger needlepoint stitch. Elaborate jeweled frame. 6 x 9. The Curiosity Shop. $395.00 – 595.00.

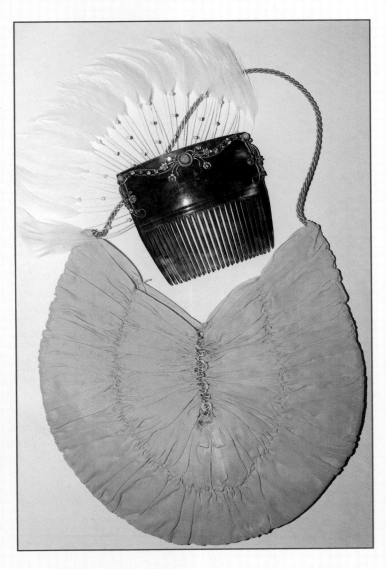

This American made purse, circa 1910 – 20, is in a classic style with a shirred crepe-like material and a decorative floral center. The material is placed around a hidden metal wire to form a partial oval. Possibly made to match a dress. 9 x 9. From the collection of Paula Higgins. $200.00 – 295.00.

A detailed petit point purse with two distinctive scenes—on the front, a servant and her mistress; on the reverse, a pair of unusual animals. Flanking swans arching their sinewy necks secure the decorative gilt frame's carry chain. 6 x 9. From the collection of Diane Goldfarb. $800.00 – 1,000.00.

Beautifully rendered petit point figural of a lady serenely musing by the water's edge in a pastoral setting. On the reverse, a young man gently frolics with his dog. Silver arched frame. 7 x 9. The Curiosity Shop. $750.00 – 950.00.

Nineteenth century American purse of white work with a netted and knotted fringe. The front depicts a vase of flowers; the back, a cornucopia. Probably made by a child or unskilled adult. 4 x 5. From the collection of Paula Higgins. $275.00 – 375.00.

Satin stitched purse with Chinese figures surrounded by unusual cord work. Lovely jeweled frame with thumb clasp opening. Circa 1930s. 6 x 7½. From the collection of Paula Higgins. $400.00 – 600.00.

Early shield shaped purse made of silk and silver metallic threads in a stylized, geometric floral design. It contains a scarlet sarcenet (a soft thin silk in plain weave) lining. The reverse of this unusual purse has a different color variation and design. Note the braided binding and handle. 5 x 7. From the collection of Paula Higgins. $450.00 – 550.00.

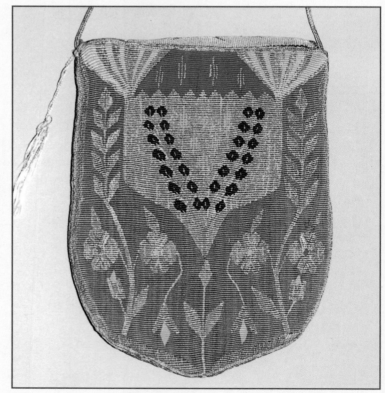

Pretty petit point floral design purse, simple frame. Second quarter of the twentieth century. 6 x 6. The Curiosity Shop. $275.00 – 375.00.

French wool needlework purse with crewel embroidery featuring a bird in a bush within a centralized floral wreath. Wool was rarely used in fine needlework due to its coarse nature. First quarter of the twentieth century. 6½ x 7½. From the collection of Paula Higgins. $400.00 – 600.00.

A late 1800s royal blue velvet purse with unique frame clasp. Matching velvet carry cord (hidden). Metal plaque on front for a monogram. 7 x 6. The Curiosity Shop. $150.00 – 275.00.

Chatelaine purses were worn proudly on the front of the dress at the waist.

French Aubusson tapestry figural purse. Of superb quality and extraordinarily vibrant color, it features two different eighteenth century French country scenes, although the purse itself is from the turn of the twentieth century. 9½ x 11. From the collection of Paula Higgins. $700.00 – 950.00.

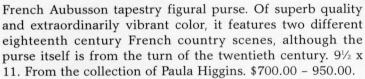

Charming nineteenth century French spider web pattern needlework purse utilizing an uncommon technique. Gilt frame is of an ornate grape and leaf design. Tiny gilt spheres form the tassel. 2¾ x 4½. From the collection of Paula Higgins. $500.00 – 800.00.

Trinity plate dance purse of black moiré, embroidered with tambour work. Green silk lining and mirror inside. From the early part of the twentieth century. 4 x 5½. From the collection of Paula Higgins. $450.00 – 650.00.

The reverse reveals a fabric covered exterior.

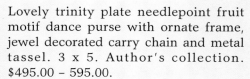

Lovely trinity plate needlepoint fruit motif dance purse with ornate frame, jewel decorated carry chain and metal tassel. 3 x 5. Author's collection. $495.00 – 595.00.

Elaborately lined with silk, it contains an attached interior mirror.

A Turkish hand-sewn export purse of chain stitched embroidered purple silk. Threads are gold, silver, bronze, and orange metallic. 4½ x 4½. From the collection of Paula Higgins. $200.00 – 400.00.

Tambour worked floral dance purse on black taffeta in dusty rose, gold, and green with an enameled and jeweled frame. 4 x 5½. From the collection of Paula Higgins. $450.00 – 650.00.

Scottish fine glass beaded envelope purse, embroidered in gold metal paillettes. On the front, a stag, birds, and flowers; on the flap, an upside down figure, probably a Chinaman; on the back, a vase of flowers — all in a stylized design. Bound in salmon silk and metallic threads, it is typical of the eighteenth century. 5 x 7. From the collection of Paula Higgins. Very rare.

A rather large, vibrantly colored, embroidered floral purse with a figural medallion flap style closure. 10 x 8. From the collection of Diane Goldfarb. $495.00 – 650.00.

Unique textured fabric combination that includes a watered silk floral pattern with black velvet stripes on either side. Combined with an art nouveau style frame, this purse dates to the early twentieth century. 6 x 9. The Curiosity Shop. $195.00 – 295.00.

Beautiful tapestry figural purse of lovers with a jewel encrusted frame embossed with cornucopias. Note the mysterious figure toward the right. Perhaps she was startled when her companion found her? 7 x 9. From the collection of Diane Goldfarb. $795.00 – 995.00.

Multi-figural petit point purse with decorative jeweled frame. 7 x 9. From the collection of Diane Goldfarb. $700.00 – 850.00.

This red jeweled gilt are well suited to the purse. 7 x 9. From the collection of Diane Goldfarb. $550.00 – 650.00.

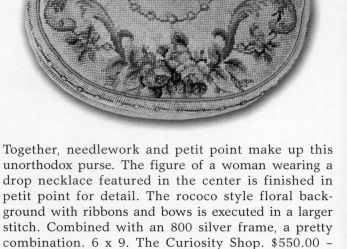

A well executed petit point purse featuring a central medallion depicting a tall vase with a generous amount of flowers spilling over the sides. The petit point artist used only the brightest colors for the subject matter for dramatic effect. The black jeweled enameled frame provides balance for the black background stitching found at the base of the bag. Notice the winged cherubs clinging to vines and peacocks balancing on branches found in the design. 7 x 10. The Curiosity Shop. $750.00 – 950.00.

Together, needlework and petit point make up this unorthodox purse. The figure of a woman wearing a drop necklace featured in the center is finished in petit point for detail. The rococo style floral background with ribbons and bows is executed in a larger stitch. Combined with an 800 silver frame, a pretty combination. 6 x 9. The Curiosity Shop. $550.00 – 750.00.

Hand-painted silk reticule in a berry and leaf pattern. Silk fringe creates a dramatic decorative effect at the top of this drawstring purse, while a silk tassel finishes the bottom. Women who made purses during this era often hand painted many decorative articles. American, early nineteenth century. From the collection of Paula Higgins. Rare.

This cream velvet "Theorem" reticule style purse uses silk cording to outline and has accent tassels of silk and chenille. It is painted using a stencil, then set with a type of gum mixture. Both sides of the purse are different. American. 8 x 8. From the collection of Paula Higgins. Very rare.

Small envelope style silk purse with silk polychrome embroidery in satin stitch. Rococo floral design, salmon colored braided trim. The lining opens to reveal eighteenth century writing on cardboard backing. Homemade purses of earlier times were occasionally fashioned with recycled materials. 4½ x 5½. From the collection of Paula Higgins. Rare.

Pretty needlework purse with jeweled and filigree encrusted frame. Colorful rose design. A portion of the scalloped filigree frame is hinged and can be flipped upward. 6 x 9½. The Curiosity Shop. $350.00 – 450.00.

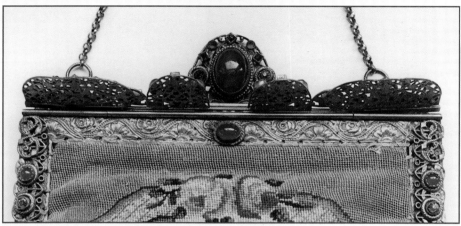

A grape harvesting scene in needlework with a simple enameled frame. The story behind the light beaming on one of the workers remains a mystery. 6 x 8. From the collection of Diane Goldfarb. $600.00 – 795.00.

Exotic bird motif figural petit point purse. Jeweled and filigree scalloped purse frame. 7 x 9½. From the collection of Diane Goldfarb. $750.00 – 850.00.

Early fine knit purse of silver metallic thread and polychrome silk in reticule form. Morning glories in a trailing pattern incorporate a bird in the design. Braided silk and metal threads finish with a beaded acorn and leaf. 6 x 10. From the collection of Paula Higgins. Rare.

An export of Turkish origin with gold metal covered thread and machine embroidery on gauze. Early artificial silk (early synthetics from about 1890 to 1920) lining. Although still an antique by today's standards, earlier styles were resurrected for years in the export business. 8 x 10. From the collection of Paula Higgins. $295.00 – 395.00.

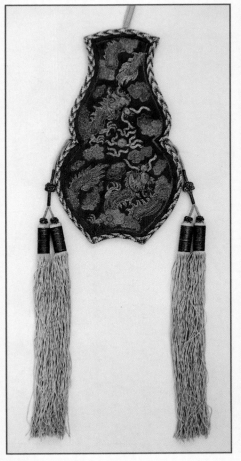

Blue silk gourd shaped pouch with raised padded dragons, their claws open. Silver and gold wrapped silk highlighted with red and green. Handmade cords have bound tassels, each with two small and one large abacus knot. Nineteenth century, China. 3¼ x 11. From the collection of Paula Higgins. $350.00 – 495.00.

Tapestry purse with pensive figural. Beautiful jeweled and enameled frame. 6½ x 9. The Curiosity Shop. $450.00 – 650.00.

Petit point purse with floral motif. Second quarter of the twentieth century. 6 x 7. The Curiosity Shop. $400.00 – 600.00.

Dance purses were suitable for use at formal affairs in the early twentieth century.

Aubusson tapestry purse with exceptional jeweled frame. Figurals depicting a romantic scene are highly sought after. The reverse shows a landscape scene. 8 x 10. From the collection of Diane Goldfarb. $800.00 – 950.00.

Plush brown velvet purse with an applied embroidered medallion on a jeweled metal filigree plate. Matching Trinity plate jeweled frame. Early twentieth century. 7 x 9. Author's collection. Rare.

Homemade late eighteenth century American-made purse with maker's name, "Amanda T. Guerig," worked into the design. Typical for the time period, a "v" was used for a "u." The middle initial is a "t" not an "f." This was accomplished using queen stitch embroidery, the most difficult embroidery stitch, no longer in use after the mid-nineteenth century. The geometric strawberry design was also typical of the day. 4 x 6. From the collection of Paula Higgins. $900.00 – 1,200.00.

The reverse side is cross stitched on canvas with queen stitch embroidery. The house depicted is most likely that of the purse maker's. Inside, the purse has a handmade fine silk lining with two divisions and an eighteenth century handmade needle secured in the middle divider. This purse is rare because of its American origin, subject matter, and the type of stitch used.

A Hobé clutch bag originally designed for the Broadway production of *My Fair Lady*. The purse ornament on the front has prong set crystals. Original accessories include mirror and change purse. Circa 1960. 7 x 8. Courtesy of Diane S. Hobé. Rare.

As spectacular as some purses may be, there are still those so unusual and exceptional that they practically defy categorization. Some of these were created from unique materials or formed into uncommon shapes. Others were designed to accommodate an unexpected accessory or were equipped with matching amenities. Still others embedded an unanticipated accessory into the purse frame itself.

Ordinarily, purses conceal their contents in a practical, fashionable manner. However, in one extreme case, a nineteenth century purse is not distinguished by the unique way in which it keeps its interior concealed; instead, the beveled glass panels deliberately showcase its remarkable contents!

This is merely a sampling of the characteristics by which these "personality" purses are judged and favored. Their uniqueness elevates them to a level above their glamorous vintage purse cousins, even by the high standards of today's collector.

A French tulip-shaped purse that appears to change colors as it moves, dating from the French Empire period, falls in this category. The unusual shape was achieved with visible curved brass ribs set into a gilt repousse floral designed base. Made from purple and gold silk, the original green silk ribbon was finished with a brass acorn anchoring its end. Brass rings are positioned on the inside where the ribbon runs through.

This chameleon-style handbag consists of ombre silk, also called changeable silk in the literature of the period because its colors seem to vary as it is moved. Because Empress Josephine loved clothing in general, and purses in particular, purse makers outdid themselves creating seldom seen designs like this. Many costume historians agree that it was one of the most creative periods in purse making history, evidenced in part by the ingenuity involved in the composition of this handbag.

Purses that incorporate accoutrements into their frames, as do watch purses, or contain them, in the form of opera glasses within a custom built purse, are certainly worthy of inclusion in this category of rare vintage purses.

Having watches as part of the purse design is a rare novelty. The watches are encased in solid jackets with protruding winding stems for easy access. It could be easily removed for repair, cleaning, or other maintenance. Often, this accessory is com-

This French tulip-shaped purse consists of ombre silk which appears to change color as it is moved. The unique shape is achieved with visible curved brass ribs set into a gilt repousse floral designed base. Made from purple and gold silk, the original green silk ribbon is anchored with a brass acorn. There are brass rings on the inside where the ribbon runs through. This chameleon style handbag dates to the French Empire period. 6 x 5½. From the collection of Paula Higgins. Very rare.

bined with purses made primarily of mesh, although examples also exist in celluloid and suede.

Over a century ago, velvet purses used almost exclusively to encase opera glass were created in a limited quantity. Made solely for the opera enthusiast, this type of purse holds a pair of ladies' opera glasses fitted perfectly within the bottom portion of the purse, accessible with the touch of a lower button. A special section is shaped for the express purpose of snugly accommodating the glasses. With the mirrored compartment fully lined, this infrequently found purse accessory is kept safe and lint free, ready for use at the next event. The purse, difficult to find without wear to the outside velvet, especially around the rigid edges, has an upper portion of the purse available for trinkets. A similar version is

Outstanding green velvet encased opera glasses purse. Made especially for the opera enthusiast, a pair of ladies' opera glasses is fitted perfectly within the bottom portion of the purse, accessible with the touch of a lower button. Fully lined, the top portion of the purse is available for trinkets. Matching carry strap, unused condition. 6 x 7. Author's collection. Rare.

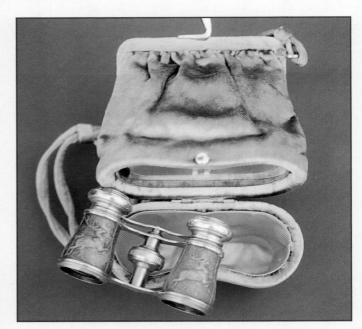

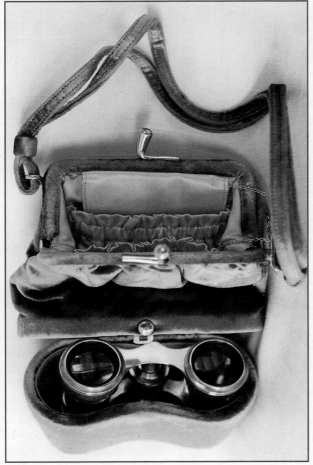

found with an additional division for a powder receptacle and puff.

A colorful silk floral purse is equipped with the matching amenity of a flowery silk fan. The fan has a ribbed celluloid handle that helps date the purse to the first quarter of the twentieth century. Since this lovely fan was stored inside the purse for years, it is evident upon comparison of materials that the sun had affected the true color of the exterior.

An unsigned nineteenth century velvet purse offers a curious display featuring beveled glass panels that invite a voyeuristic inspection of its interior. Instead of discreetly hiding its contents, this bag boldly beckons scrutiny. Extravagantly fitted with cut glass perfume bottles and droppers, it is equipped with an added bonus — a working musical box. Gilded brass fittings decorate the carry handle as well as the tasseled sides. Suitable for upper class travel needs, the fragile contents have amazingly survived without damage through many decades.

Purses with a famous provenance are a rare discovery. One such late eighteenth century basket-style bag with a fascinating history was

A colorful silk floral purse is equipped with the matching amenity of a flowery silk fan. The fan has a ribbed celluloid handle that helps date the purse to the first quarter of the twentieth century. Since this lovely fan was stored inside the purse for years, it is evident upon comparison of materials that the sun had affected the true color of the exterior. While it is unusual for a silk purse to have a metal tassel, this one is original. 6 x 12. Author's collection. $295.00 – 395.00.

An unsigned nineteenth century velvet purse offers a curious display featuring beveled glass panels that invite a voyeuristic inspection of its interior. Instead of discreetly hiding its contents, this bag boldly beckons scrutiny. Extravagantly fitted with cut glass perfume bottles and droppers, it is equipped with an added bonus — a working musical box. Gilded brass fittings decorate the carry handle as well as the tasseled sides. Suitable for upper class travel needs, the fragile contents have amazingly survived without damage through many decades. 6½ x 6½. Author's collection. Rare.

Leather umbrella purses with gate top frames. The frame expands to allow access to the small purse. When closed the frame lid snaps over the hinges. The one on the right has a hook to attach to a chatelaine or belt. 2 x 4. Author's collection. $225.00 – 375.00 each.

originally designed to hold needlework. It evolved from a needlework holder into a roomy reticule that held a smaller purse, letters, smelling salt containers, knotting shuttles, and the like. The top of the bag is made of blue chenille thread and silver gilt with a netted design. Blue and white silk ribbons form the drawstring, which are finished in matching silver gilt. The octagonal base is constructed of blue silk embroidery in gilded threads with a floral motif. The underside is trimmed using silver and gold braid.

This reticule, owned by Edward Austen Knight, brother of the famous late eighteenth and early nineteenth century writer, Jane Austen, was probably purchased for his wife, Elizabeth, around the time of their wedding in 1791. Thomas Knight II adopted Edward Austen Knight at the age of 16. He used the name Austen until his adoptive father died, at which time he added Knight's last name. It was customary for inheritances to travel through male ancestral lines during the eighteenth century, consequently making him quite wealthy upon his father's death. He ultimately gave a house (called Chawton Cottage) to his sister, Jane Austen, to live in for the last eight years of her life. He still owned the purse, while living in Chawton Great House, next door.

Despite having eleven potential heirs with his wife Elizabeth, Christie's of London eventually auctioned the purse in 1992.

In the early twentieth century, complexly stitched French velvet purses with couched metallic gold threads and tiny faux pearls were made with such detail that it is obvious they were best suited for formal occasions such as balls, weddings, receptions, or the opera. Intricately fashioned, gold thread and a row of pearls adorns the gusset of one such handbag. It is topped with an elaborately jeweled frame. Such care and detail was given to its creation that there was even extra time spent to produce a matching change purse to fit securely in the rich, silk-lined pocket. Long ago, it was given to a faithful restaurant employee in Pennsylvania after many years of devoted service.

Before celluloid was invented, purse designers were sometimes forced to use unorthodox materials to create an accessory that stood out from the rest. One of the known sources in use at the time was tortoise shell, a natural plastic derived from the hawksbill turtle. It could be heated and molded, then shaped or cut into many forms. Such was the case with a nineteenth century vintage French tortoise-shell and gold leather embossed purse with a steel

This late eighteenth century basket style bag was originally designed to hold needlework but evolved into a roomy reticule that held a smaller purse, letters, smelling salts containers, knotting shuttles, and the like. The top of the bag is made of blue chenille thread and silver gilt with a netted design. Blue and white silk ribbons form the drawstring, which are finished in matching silver gilt. 8 x 10. From the collection of Paula Higgins. Very rare.

Blue silk forms the octagonal base, embroidered in gilt threads with a floral design. The bottom is trimmed using silver gilt braid.

Owned by Edward Austen Knight, brother of the famous late eighteenth–early nineteenth century writer, Jane Austen. It was probably purchased for his wife, Elizabeth, around the time of their wedding in 1791. The purse was eventually auctioned by Christie's in London in 1992.

A charming glass beaded floral design within a square border resembles a framed picture that might be placed on a wall. The jeweled frame incorporates oval faux carnelian cabochons. 7 x 10. Author's collection. $800.00 – 1,000.00.

___

clasp in the shape of a lyre. Obviously a gift for a special someone, the reverse has an elliptical plaque embossed with the word "souvenir," which translates to "remember me."

Another material eventually replaced with celluloid was ivory. An unlikely source — painted paper (covering card) — was fabricated to look like ivory as it formed the body of a very distinguished purse from the 1830s. A genuine carved ivory leaf and grape appliqué with a green China silk reticule top adds to its striking design. With corded tassels on both sides, a quatrefoil knotted theme finishes the presentation.

Jewel encrusted metal dance purses, often marked "Trinity Plate," were made in the 1920s. Those found with the original metal fringe tassel and ornate or jeweled carry chains add appreciably to their value. Fashioned in various shapes — rectangular, octagonal, and round — many have filigree work or incorporate a needlework medallion as part of the design. These small bags were elegantly draped on the arm while maneuvering the dance floor in the

Roaring Twenties, the tassels swaying in time with the fringe and beads on fancy dresses.

Around the turn of the twentieth century, dual personality purses incorporated a scenic, floral, or figural petit point insert within a glass beaded border. This is usually combined with a silk stitched landscape scene on the reverse, which is also inset within a glass beaded border (although there are known examples where the reverse may be comprised entirely of glass beads). Below are instructions for a 1920s version as it appeared in *A Distinctive Group of Beaded Bags*, published in 1925:

"THE ALAMAC" Model No. 253

MATERIALS:
4 Bunches "Hiawatha" Flame-Glo Gems No. 37
9 Dozen "Hiawatha" Jewels No. 2731 or 2530
1 Hiawatha" Bag Frame No. 6213/5
1 Pair "Hiawatha" Knitting Pins No. 15
1 Spool Purse Twist
1 Pair "Hiawatha" Knit Pin Protectors No. 93
2 "Hiawatha" Petit Point Squares No. 3449

"The Alamac," a combination beaded/petit point purse with detailed instructions to make it, appeared in the Dritz-Traum Company's booklet. *A Distinctive Group of Beaded Bags*, 1925.

This bag, unique in appearance, is especially designed to represent the fashionable needlepoint bags which are so popular.

Size of Bag: Width at top, 4 inches, at bottom, 6 inches. Length, 6½ inches.

Instructions: Cast on 35 st loosely. Knit back plain. K 2 ridges pl (no beads).

Note: Always knit back plain (no beads) on inside of bag.

Ridge 3: K 3 st, sl 1 b, k l, sl 1, etc., finishing R. with 3 pl st.

Ridges 4 to 12: Same as Ridge 3.

Ridge 13: Same as Ridge 3 except cast on 2 st on each end of needle.

Ridge 14: Same as Ridge 13 except cast on 2 st on each end of needle (making 43 st in all).

Ridge 15: Same as Ridge 14.

Ridge 16: K 2, sl b, k 1, for 8 b, k 25 st pl, sl b, k 1 for 8 b, k 2 pl.

Ridge 17: K 1, sl b, for 9 b, k 25 pl sl b, k 1 for 9 b, k 1 pl, k back 12 st pl. Bind off 19 st loosely. K 12 st pl.

Ridge 18: K 1, sl 1 for 9 b, k 3 pl. Take off the 12 st on other end of needle onto a safety pin. K back pl on first 12 st. K 20 R. same as 18th R., making 21 R. in all. Do not knit back on the 21st R. but take it off on a safety pin and cut thread. Take up the other side and knit 21 R. (same as on other side). Knit back pl on this side-cast on 19 st loosely and knit on the other 12 st (making 43 st needle).

Ridge 39: K 1, sl bead for 9 b, k 25 st pl, sl b, k 1, etc., to end. K back plain.

Ridge 40: Same as Ridge 39.

Ridge 41: K 1, sl b, etc., to end. Knit back plain.

Ridge 42: Same as Ridge 41, but decrease 1 st on each end of needle when knitting back.

Ridge 43: K 40 b, decreasing 1 pl st on each end when knitting back.

Ridge 44: Same as 43rd R. only knitting 38B.

Ridge 45: Same as 43rd R. only knitting 36B.

Ridge 46: Same as 43rd R. only knitting 34B.

Ridge 47: Same as 43rd R. only knitting 32B. When knitting back, bind off first 3 st. Continue pl.

Ridge 48: Bind off first 3 st k 1 sl b, etc., to end, making 26 b in row.

Bind off first 3 st when knitting back.

Ridge 49: Bind off first 3 st sl b, etc., making 20 b in row. Knit back pl. Bind off. This completes one half the bag. Make the other half in exactly the same manner.

Mount petit point pieces on crinolin, and sew 1 piece in each open square in center of bag. Sew jewels around edge of petit point pieces (where plain stitches are knitted). Sew sides of bag together leaving opening at top for frame.

Lining and Mounting: Mount frame and line bag with silk.

In the nineteenth century, calling card cases were frequently used to hold their namesake and, on occasion, a small amount of money. During this era, when visitors came to call, they simply left their cards in or near the entranceway as evidence that they had come to visit. Conveniently small in stature, the central portion of a mother of pearl example depicts a European woman in a country setting, possibly harvesting hay, surrounded by ornate scroll work.

A French tortoiseshell and gold leather embossed purse with a steel clasp in the shape of a lyre. Obviously a gift for a special someone, the reverse has an elliptical plaque embossed with the word, "souvenir," which translates to remember me. Circa 1800. 6¼ x 5¼. From the collection of Paula Higgins. $2,000.00+.

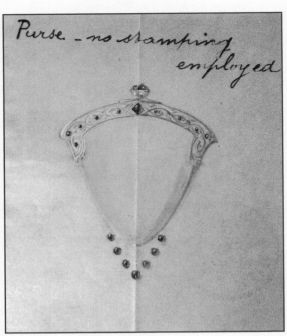

Unusual artist colored purse design drawings from the early first quarter of the twentieth century. Courtesy of the Napier Company archives.

A raspberry vine against an unusual teal blue glass beaded background is a winning recipe for producing a rare purse. 7 x 12. Author's collection. Rare.

Grape and grape vine motif purse in tiny glass beads. Reticule top with a draw string pull closure. 8 x 13. Author's collection. 1,500.00 +.

Mary Pickford stands on the front porch stairs at her place of birth in Toronto.

An intricately stitched French velvet purse featuring hand laid and couched metallic gold threads and tiny faux pearls. Suitable for a formal occasion such as a ball, wedding, reception, or opera. A row of pearls and gold thread adorn the gusset and it is topped with an elaborately jeweled frame. A matching change purse fitting snugly in the rich silk-lined pocket is evidence that tremendous care and detail was given to the purse's creation. Long ago, this purse was given to a faithful restaurant employee in Pennsylvania after many years of devoted service. Early twentieth century. 7 x 9. Author's collection, borrowed by bride Carol Sullivan. $495.00 – 695.00.

Bombe shaped faux ivory body and genuine carved ivory leaf and grape appliqué with China silk reticule top, green braid trim. Corded tassels on sides with quatrefoil shaped knots. Circa 1830. 6 x 10. From the collection of Paula Higgins. Very rare.

Intricate small purse designs from 1911 and 1912. Courtesy of the Napier Company archives.

Jewel encrusted filigree metal dance purse. The original tassel and ornate linked carry chain is still present, adding to its value. These small bags were suitably draped on the arm while maneuvering the dance floor in the Roaring Twenties, the tassels swaying in time with the fringe and beads on fancy dresses. Marked "Trinity Plate." 3 x 5½. Author's collection. $375.00 – 495.00.

A jewel clasp dance purse with a pretty petit point stitched floral front. The interior is of beige silk with shirred pockets that include a small wallet. 3 x 5. The Curiosity Shop. $350.00 – 495.00.

Octagonal shaped trinity plate dance purse with bezel set jewels surrounding a needlework floral medallion. Jeweled carry chain and metal tassel. 3 x 3. The Curiosity Shop. $350.00 – 495.00.

Art Deco brown suede purse with ornate marcasite and carnelian encrusted watch overclasp in sterling. The suede body of the bag cleverly conceals the frame. The interior is accessed by lifting the entire watch section. 5 x 9. The Curiosity Shop. Rare.

A working timepiece is incorporated into the wide embossed frame of a ring mesh purse. 6 x 7. The Curiosity Shop. Rare.

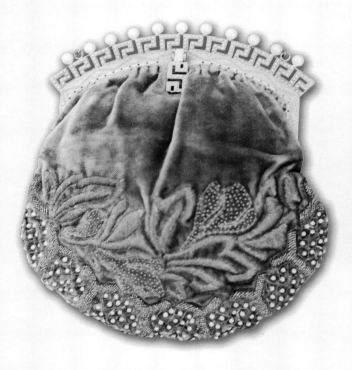

Early twentieth century French velvet traditional pouch shaped purse, with intricate metallic gold stitching in a leaf design. Faux pearls are sewn along the gusset portion of the bag. Ornate Greek key designed frame, crown set with faux pearls. 7 x 9. The Curiosity Shop. $350.00 – 450.00.

Hindeloopen

12663

COPR. DETROIT PUBLISHING CO.

American figural/scenic purse. Home-crafted bag of beads on leather along with appliqué foil back cabochons. On one side, two ornate birds grasp a shield with their talons, displaying the initials "J.P." On the reverse, an equally imaginative butterfly in beads. Looped fringe all around, tassel, and beaded twisted carry strap. 1920s. 9 x 7½. The Curiosity Shop. $650.00 – 800.00.

Unique combination of a silk stitched figural scene of a woman reading a book set within a floral glass beaded border. A silk landscape scene is shown on the reverse, also surrounded by a glass beaded border. Twisted loop fringe. 7 x 10. The Curiosity Shop. Rare.

Made in France — tiny glass beads form a carpet motif purse. The crown type jeweled frame over clasp is an added attraction. 9 x 13. Author's collection. $1,200.00 + .

Mother of pearl calling card case, also used to carry money, with a three sectional interior. The central exterior portion of the purse depicts a European woman, possibly harvesting hay, surrounded by ornate scroll work. When friends and acquaintances came to call, they would simply leave their calling cards, in or near the entranceway, indicating that they had come to visit. Mid to late nineteenth century. 2½ x 4. From the collection of Paula Higgins. $295.00 – 395.00.

Tortoiseshell purse with 14k pique work and mother of pearl inlay. Four sectional silk interior. Mid to late 1800s. 2½ x 4. From the collection of Paula Higgins. $350.00 – 450.00.

1913. Courtesy of the Napier Company archives.

An ornate filigree medallion decorates this unusual jeweled fabric dance purse. It has an underlying metal form for shape. The interior is lined with pockets for storage. 6 x 6. Author's collection. $500.00 – 650.00.

Tortoiseshell purse with gilt appliqué in an arabesque pattern. Mid to late nineteenth century. 2 x 4. From the collection of Paula Higgins. $295.00 – 395.00.

1930s American tooled leather purse with peacock motif combined with a butterscotch colored Bakelite handle and clasp. Birds and animals are not commonly found on leather purses. 8 x 9. From the collection of Paula Higgins. $225.00 – 325.00.

Surrounded by plush velvet, the focal point, a jeweled petit point floral appliqué, matches the frame. Shown open to reveal a rich silk interior with shirred pocket and matching mirror. 7 x 7. Author's collection. Rare.

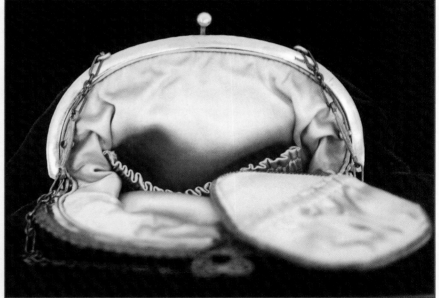

Innovative designs that incorporate powder compacts into purses in unanticipated ways are a delight and challenge to find, whether the compacts are part of the frame or are connected by virtue of the carry chain. These types of purses are called vanity bags or compact purses. Their collectibility is two-fold, as they are sought by both compact collectors and purse enthusiasts.

The artistic methods companies employed as they integrated powder compacts and purses are chronicled. This astounding manufacturing ingenuity includes a wide range of variety that places the compact within an oval, rectangle, square, or circular shape at the very top of the frame. They can also be integrated in the central portion of the bag, with mesh above and below it, as is the case of the rare Delysia. Likewise, they can be found attached to the sides of the purse frame, resembling the dual vanity purse called The New Piccadilly.

A Whiting and Davis vanity bag with a front side compact called a Corner Compact Costume Bag. Combined with a scenic Dresden style fine mesh body, this compact purse is a rarity. 5½ x 8. From the collection of Elaine Lehn. Very rare.

Innovative designs that incorporate the compact into the purse in unusual ways are a delight to find, whether they are part of the frame or connected to the carry chain.

Compacts are also found on the front side of the purse, like the Corner Compact Bag, or attached to the frame, but suspended below the front center, comparable to the rare Swinging Compact Costume Purse. Compacts are also attached at the very bottom, similar to the Evans black fabric bag from the mid-twentieth century, or attached to the carry chain, like The DuBarry Bag. In fact, compacts have been attached to purses in almost every conceivable way!

The flat enameled mesh Corner Compact Costume Bag, made by the largest manufacturer of vanity purses, Whiting and Davis, is an example of how an enameled compact is attached to the frame on the front side. Once opened, the powder cavity and

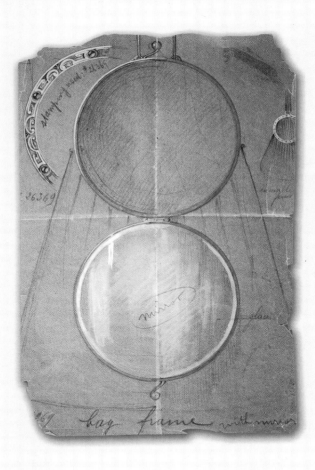

Design drawing for a mesh purse containing a vanity mirror. January, 1913. Courtesy of the Napier Company archives, photograph by Walter Kitik.

In the tradition of a trinity-plated compact, this unusual jewel encrusted purse has a compact located on the front. Notice the jeweled carry chain and matching tassel. 3¼ x 4. From the collection of Diane Goldfarb. $650.00 – 850.00.

Ornate gilt filigree metal, jewel encrusted vanity purse with metal tassel. Front lid opens to reveal mirror, powder cavity, and puff. The interior is lined with pockets. 4½ x 4½. Author's collection. $650.00 – 850.00.

---

mirror can be accessed. Another one of their innovations, called the Swinging Compact Costume Purse, contains the compact centered on the frame. Instead of sitting rigidly in place, the compact swings on a hinge. These purses were expensive to produce and were not made in quantity.

An El-Sah has a rectangular shaped compact as part of the frame. Compact lids have enameled floral designs, jewels, or black silhouetted scenes of a man and woman in dance pose. Access to the compact portion is gained when the thumb piece is depressed and the lid lifted up. There are slight variations in interiors. Either a powder and rouge cavity with powder puffs is present along with an oval mirror with a comb holder, or there is an area for calling cards or cigarettes along with a powder area. Lifting

---

An oval French red celluloid compact purse with embedded jewels. On each side, an elegant swan with an arched neck captures the carry cord. Shown open to reveal a lipstick and powder puff. 3½ x 4½. The Curiosity Shop. $300.00 – 400.00.

the entire compact section attains entrance to the purse portion. Here, there is room for some small items such as a hankie, money, or other trinkets.

Whiting and Davis also produced the compact purse, The Delysia. It was available in two mesh varieties: fine ring and flat enameled mesh. The most striking feature of this vanity bag, aside from the fact that it resembles a hanging Christmas tree ornament, is that the compact is nestled in the center of the purse. When opened, a hinged arm holding the powder puff to the powder receptacle is shown. It also contains a rouge pot and two mirrors. Available in the early 1920s, it exists in three sizes: 2", 2½", and 3". For the finishing touch, a tassel is composed of flat mesh link, fine ring mesh, or black silk.

The Baby Peggy was a smaller version of the Delysia vanity bag. An advertisement dated 1924, reads "for her daughter, in gold, silver, or colored enameled with silken top." This silk-topped variation of The Delysia was made without a compact, thereby keeping the manufacturing cost down for the Whiting and Davis Company.

A purse called The New Piccadilly, was a dual compact purse advertised by Whiting and Davis as "more practical" than beads with a large "loose-pact" (sifter style) powder and rouge compartment with mirror. The Piccadilly style vanity bag was more commonly available. It incorporated a small round compact at the central top portion of the frame, visible on the front of the purse. The frame

is in the shape of a wishbone; the purse is of the fine ring mesh variety.

The Evans Case Company was incorporated in 1922, in North Attleboro, Massachusetts. They produced mesh vanity purses, compacts with fabric pouches, and purses fitted with compacts, jewelry, and other vanity items. Two of their most popular and widely available vanity purses had a round gold-plated or enameled top combined with a flat mesh goldtone pouch. Another style contained an oval compact lid with enameling, incorporating a delicate floral design. On occasion, one of their tango chain purses (lipstick attached to the compact with a short link connector chain) is encountered.

Infrequently, Evans utilized beadlite mesh. When this raised metal dot in the center of a flat link is enameled in color, it emulates glass or steel beading. Also manufactured were fabric purses fitted with compacts, mirrors, and combs. The Evans insignia can be found sewn into the linings.

The Bliss Napier Company, founded in 1875, carried a varied product line that included jewelry, novelties, sterling silver giftware, compacts, purses, and vanity bags. In the spring of 1921, the company introduced The DuBarry Purse. This vanity bag has an embossed, arched frame in the form of an inverted "V" and a fine ring mesh body. The artistically designed powder case is attached in an innovative way to the braided mesh carry strap instead of being integrated into the frame.

The DuBarry was first introduced to jewelry wholesalers through trade magazines. Once it debuted there, it was formally introduced in the pages of *Vogue* magazine in order to reach the retail buyer. The purse was made during the Bliss tenure, before the name was changed to Napier, and was stamped accordingly inside the frame.

Theodore W. Foster & Brothers Company (F&B) began business in 1873 with the main office and factory located in Providence, Rhode Island. They were manufacturing jewelers and silversmiths, producing a beautiful selection of dresser sets, fobs, lorgnettes, jewelry, hand mirrors, perfume holders, vanity purses, and powder compacts. Their quality workmanship, which included sterling silver, engine turned, enameled, gilt finished, and gold filled vanity purses, quickly led to the expansion of offices in New York, Chicago, and Los Angeles.

Two of the vanity purses manufactured include The Oriental and The Romantic. Both are cylinder shaped, sterling receptacles with enameled lids that open to reveal powder compacts. The Romantic has a narrow bottom consisting of a cologne vial. The Oriental has a larger receptacle for accommodating cigarettes. These imaginative designs from 1925 also include lipsticks attached with a carry cord. Of extremely high quality, the compact purses are marked "Sterling" along with

Miniature celluloid vanity purse in black and ivory, containing a mirror. 3½ x 5. Author's collection, photograph by Irene Clarke. $175.00 – 275.00.

Silhouetted figures in a dance pose adorn this compact top. A fine ring mesh purse body by Whiting and Davis completes this vanity bag. 4 x 8. The Curiosity Shop. $800.00 – 1,000.00.

Rare enameled mesh Whiting and Davis vanity purse with jewel encrusted lid. Interior opens to reveal powder and rouge pots, powder puffs, and a square beveled glass mirror. 4 x 8. Author's collection. $1,000.00 – 1,250.00.

Whiting and Davis El-Sah enameled mesh purse with floral design lid. The top opens to reveal rouge and powder cavities, along with an oval mirror and comb holder (some still contain a Bakelite comb). 4 x 8. The Curiosity Shop. $800.00 – 1,000.00.

The Ladies' Home Journal, 1922.

the registered trademark consisting of a flag with the letters "F&B." Extraordinary attention to detail includes engine turned cases and extra long silk fringe able to conceal the entire receptacle portion.

The R&G Company produced vanity purses of quality consisting of sterling silver enameled compact lids with elaborately enameled flowers and foliage in pastel colors in the 1920s. Sturdy wrist straps are made of foxtail mesh or tightly woven braid. Inside, a round or octagon compact section has a mirror and a large receptacle for packed powder. Above the powder on the inside of the lid is a rouge pot behind a generous sized mirror.

Below the metal powder container, accessible by lifting the compact section, is a spacious mesh purse. The metal bands around the outside of the compact are embossed in silver flowers. Elaborately enameled or plain armor mesh purses by R&G were available in fine quality baby flat mesh links, half the size of standard flat mesh. The purses are embellished with metal link tassels often enameled

to match the pouches. Fashionably draped over the arm and adjusted securely by a mesh wrist strap, it offered little interference to the fancy dance stepping of the big band sound that was so popular at this time. It is marked "Sterling" along with the letters "R&G."

Other types of vanity purses include those made of Bakelite, celluloid, and other early plastics. For instance, a bolster shaped early plastic necessaire unscrews at the top and bottom to reveal a mirror, puff, powder, and rouge cavity, and a receptacle for small items. Made in the 1920s, it included a carry cord and fringed tassel. The tassel could conceal a lipstick tube, thereby saving space in these small purses for rouge and powder.

Whatever the type of vintage vanity purse, theirs is a novelty and conversation piece reflective of the fashionable eras in which they were manufactured. Whether to simply save space or provide the cutting edge of design, these once neoteric approaches to style are revitalized through the passion of collecting.

Rare enameled mesh purse, unsigned, but most likely Whiting and Davis. The compact is in the top center of the purse, and when opened, reveals a powder cavity and place for a mirror. 5½ x 8½. Author's collection. Rare.

Ring mesh purse with enameled vanity lid depicting a lounging cherub. 3½ x 4. From the collection of Diane Goldfarb. Rare.

Striking enameled mesh purse with round compact top. The lid is decorated with a thin border of blue and black to match the purse. Adjustable foxtail mesh carry strap, unsigned. 5 x 8. The Curiosity Shop. $500.00 – 700.00.

Another example of the round compact top purse, this one in fine ring mesh with a fancy fringe. 5 x 8. The Curiosity Shop. $450.00 – 650.00.

Mother could afford to purchase The Baby Peggy purse for her daughter. This silk topped variation of The Delysia is without a compact, which kept the manufacturing cost down for the Whiting and Davis Company.

The Baby Peggy, a small version of the Delysia vanity bag by Whiting and Davis. An advertisement, dated 1924, reads "for her daughter, in gold, silver, or colored enameled with silken top." 3 x 5. From the collection of Elaine Lehn. $800.00 – 1,000.00.

Advertisement for The Delysia vanity purse by Whiting and Davis. Courtesy of the Napier Company archives.

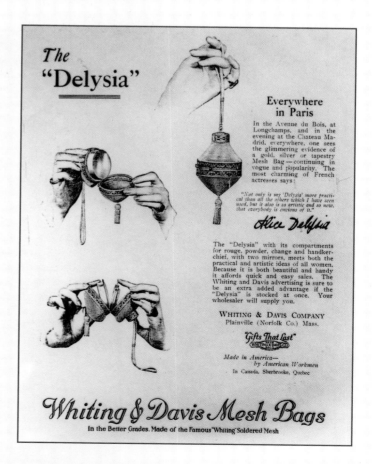

The "Delysia"

Everywhere in Paris

In the Avenue du Bois, at Longchamps, and in the evening at the Chateau Madrid, everywhere, one sees the glimmering evidence of a gold, silver or tapestry Mesh Bag—continuing in vogue and popularity. The most charming of French actresses says:

"Not only is my 'Delysia' more practical than all the others which I have seen used, but it also is so artistic and so new, that everybody is envious of it."

Alice Delysia

The "Delysia" with its compartments for rouge, powder, change and handkerchief, with two mirrors, meets both the practical and artistic ideas of all women. Because it is both beautiful and handy it affords quick and easy sales. The Whiting and Davis advertising is sure to be an extra added advantage if the "Delysia" is stocked at once. Your wholesaler will supply you.

WHITING & DAVIS COMPANY
Plainville (Norfolk Co.) Mass.

"Gifts That Last"

*Made in America—
by American Workmen*
In Canada, Sherbrooke, Quebec

Whiting & Davis Mesh Bags
In the Better Grades. Made of the Famous "Whiting" Soldered Mesh

The Delysia, a compact purse in fine ring mesh. Shown open, it displays a compact nestled in the center with the hinged arm holding a powder puff. 3 x 6. The Curiosity Shop. $1,000.00 – 1,200.00+.

Goldtone fine ring mesh Delysia purse. 3 x 6. Author's collection. $1,000.00 – 1,200.00+.

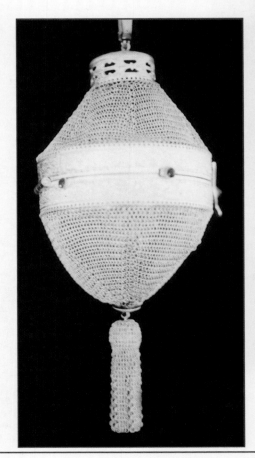

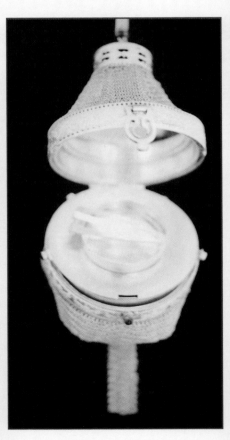

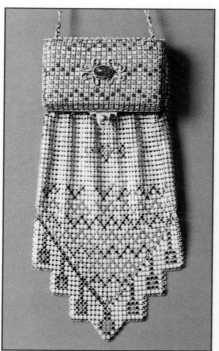

A mesh Whiting and Davis vanity purse with an enamel and jewel encrusted lid. The interior opens to reveal powder and rouge pots, powder puffs, and a beveled glass mirror. These rectangular top vanity bags were available in many color varieties and pattern styles. 4 x 8. The Curiosity Shop. $1,000.00 – 1,200.00.

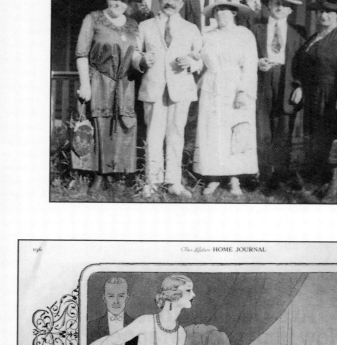

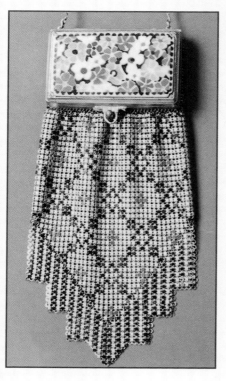

Whiting and Davis enameled mesh purse with an enameled floral pattern compact top. 4 x 8. The Curiosity Shop. $800.00 – 1,000.00.

This final touch of color
makes the prettiest gown *exquisite*

The Ladies' Home Journal.

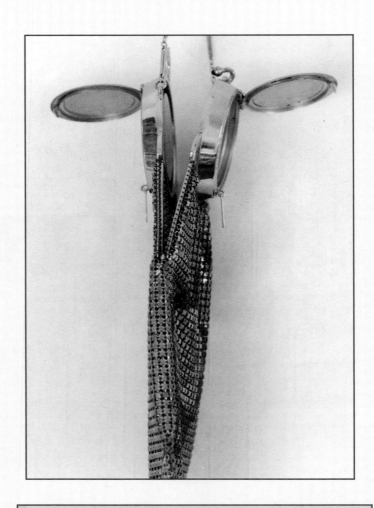

Called The New Piccadilly, this dual compact purse was advertised by Whiting and Davis as "more practical" than beads. It has a large "loose-pact" (sifter style) powder and rouge compartment with mirror. 3 x 10. Author's collection. Very rare.

Advertisement for The New Piccadilly, featuring loose-pact and rouge-pact dual openings. Courtesy of the Napier Company archives.

This version of The New Piccadilly by Whiting and Davis has a dual jewel encrusted lid and multicolored enameled mesh links. Shown open, revealing the rouge and mirror section. 3 x 10. Anonymous collector. Very rare.

The powder sifter (also known as "loose-pact") is revealed. A close-up shows the filigree and jewel detail of the lid.

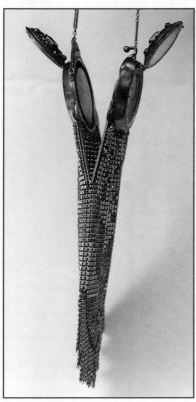

A side angle offers a view of both the rouge and powder receptacles.

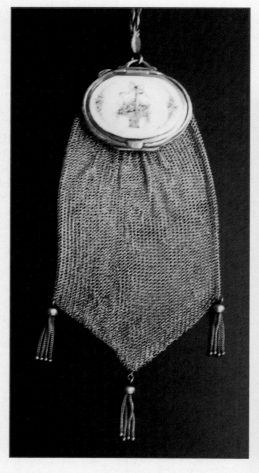

A delicate enameled flower basket in sterling with a triple tasseled finish. Shown open to reveal powder cavity, mirror, and powder puff. 3 x 7. The Curiosity Shop. $850.00 – 1,000.00.

The Piccadilly. *The Saturday Evening Post*, 1922.

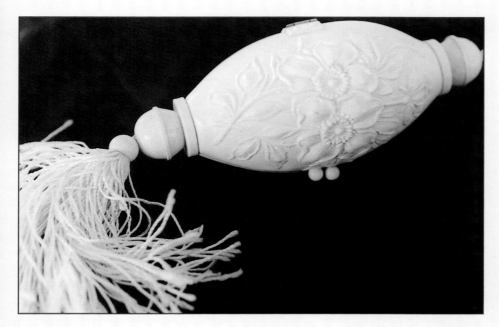

Celluloid vanity purse with raised floral design, silk cord, and tassel. 3½ x 5. The Curiosity Shop. $300.00 – 400.00.

Green early plastic vanity with green embedded stones. 3½ x 5. The Curiosity Shop. $350.00 – 450.00.

Uniquely shaped Bakelite bag with interior mirror. Black silk carry cord and tassel, red glass jewels. 2½ x 4. Author's collection. $400.00 – 600.00.

Bolster-shaped early plastic vanity case. The vanity case unscrews at the top and bottom to reveal a mirror, puff, powder, and rouge cavity, with a receptacle for sundries. Circa 1920s. 1½ x 3½. The Curiosity Shop. $600.00 – 800.00.

Ivorytone flat enameled mesh Corner Compact Costume Bag by Whiting and Davis. The enameled compact is attached to the frame on the side in the front. Shown open, the powder cavity and mirror area is revealed. 4½ x 6½. The Curiosity Shop. Very rare.

Bolster-shaped compacts from the 1920s usually came with a carry cord and fringed tassel. The tassel could conceal a lipstick tube, thereby saving space in these small purses for rouge and powder.

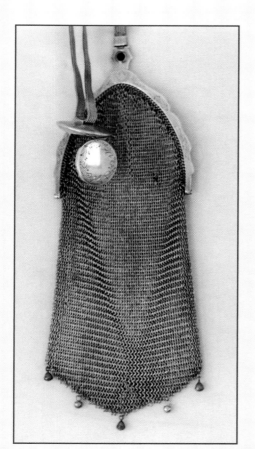

Soldered mesh vanity purse with scalloped frame. A foxtail mesh adjustable wrist chain holds an attached compact. 3½ x 7. The Curiosity Shop. $400.00 – 600.00.

THE COUNTRY KID EXPERIMENTING

CO.-F.G.H.

Announcing the Du Barry Bag

The DuBarry Bag is the perfect combination mesh bag and powder box. The exquisitely carved powder case is attached to the braided strap of the mesh bag, and when not in use, lies in the palm of the hand, thus affording a convenient way of carrying the bag.

The workmanship of the DuBarry bag is characteristic of all Napier-Bliss jewelry, and stamps it at once as a bag for the discriminating woman who appreciates the value of correct dress accessories.

The DuBarry bag comes in 14 Kt. green gold, 14 Kt. gold filled 1/10, sterling silver, and Nile-gold. It is being nationally advertised. Watch for the DuBarry bag in the May 15th issue of Vogue.

THE NAPIER-BLISS COMPANY
366 Fifth Avenue, N. Y.
Main Office and Works, MERIDEN, CONN.
Established 1875   20 Rue d'Hauteville, Paris

BLISS
Registered Trade Mark

The Bliss/Napier DuBarry Bag features a compact attached to the carry chain instead of the frame. 1921. Courtesy of the Napier Company archives.

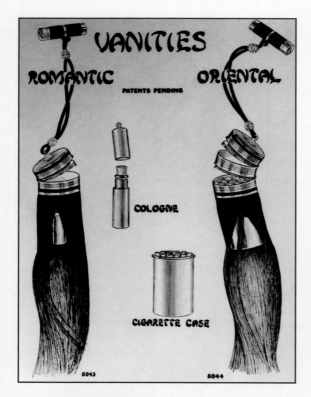

Imaginative vanity purse designs by the Theodore W. Foster & Brothers Company. Of extremely high quality, they are marked "Sterling" along with their registered trademark — a flag with the letters "F&B." Extraordinary attention to detail includes engine-turned cases and extra long silk fringe that can completely conceal the entire purse portion. *The Foster Blue Book*, 1925.

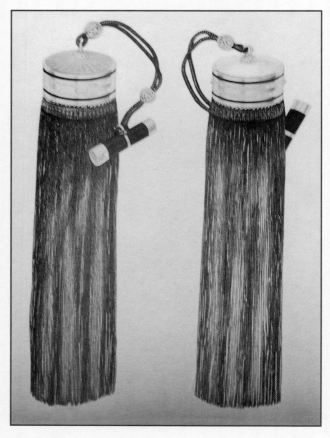

Sterling silver F&B compact purses in orange and ivory. Both colors were available in the Romantic and Oriental styles. *The Foster Blue Book*, 1925.

The manufacturing plant of the Theodore W. Foster & Brothers Company as it appeared in 1925 in Providence, Rhode Island. *The Foster Blue Book*.

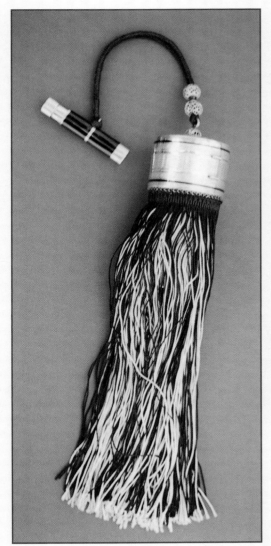

Engine-turned orchid enameled sterling silver F&B vanity purse. Known as The Oriental, it has a compartment for powder, rouge, and puffs on top with a double swinging mirror. Contains a black silk cord and ball side with a black opaque enameled lipstick on the end. The engine-turned cigarette case is concealed by orchid and black silk fringe. Memo tablet in cover. Including fringe, 1¾ x 8½. Author's collection. Very rare.

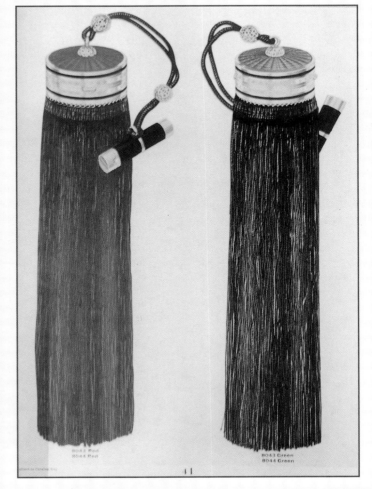

F&B vanity purse in red and green. Originally, The Romantic sold wholesale for $50.00 and The Oriental for $60.00. This was considered a large sum of money at the time. *The Foster Blue Book*, 1925.

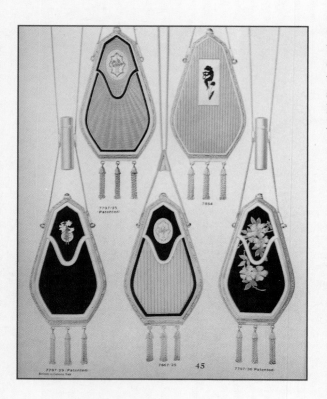

Catalog advertisement for elaborately enameled pear-shaped vanities by the F&B Company. Complete with chain tassels and attached lipsticks, the lip rouge is found in the interior along with a mirror, a memorandum tablet, and space for bills on one side; compartments for powder puff and rouge on the other. Prices ranged from $62.00 to $90.00, wholesale. *The Foster Blue Book*, 1925.

French celluloid dual opening compact with concealed lipstick in tassel and rhinestones embedded into the cover. 2 x 4. The Curiosity Shop. $300.00 – 450.00.

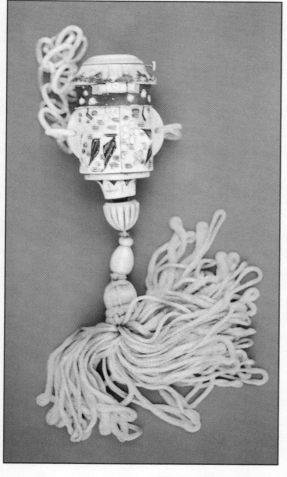

Deeply carved Bakelite vanity purse with a timepiece housed on the compact lid. Shown open, the compact portion on top is accessed and the hinged storage compartment opens from the center with a pull of the silk tassel below. 2 x 4. Author's collection. Rare.

Recently enjoying resurgence in popularity, quality purse frames (particularly those constructed from the 1800s to the 1930s) are sought by top purse collectors and are equally in demand by new handbag designers to create stunning complements for luxurious bags.

Vintage frames were constructed using a variety of materials, including celluloid, ivory, bone, tortoise, wood, and Bakelite, all of which will be discussed in another chapter. Here, the focus lies on metal varieties. Often, gold-plated brass and cast white metal frames were set with glimmering glass stones imported predominately from Czechoslovakia, Austria, France, or Germany. The faux jewels arrived in the United States in folded paper packets with tissue inserts. Sold by the gross, they were available in a variety of shapes and colors. Those with polished, domed tops are called cabochons, while faceted stones are identified by shape — roundel, baguette, oval, etc. Measured in millimeters, certain glass jewels have foil on their undersides. This special finishing process allows more light to be reflected through the sparkling faux gemstone.

Distinctive frames made of genuine precious and semi-precious stones are a formidable task to find, as they could not be produced in quantity. Amethysts, diamonds, malachite, tiger-eye, onyx, and virtually all types of gems embellish them. Ordinarily, sterling silver or copper was the chosen metal when frames were enameled. This was a lengthy, expensive process that was not wasted on inferior frames.

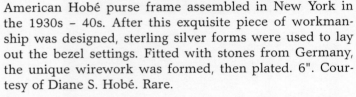

American Hobé purse frame assembled in New York in the 1930s – 40s. After this exquisite piece of workmanship was designed, sterling silver forms were used to lay out the bezel settings. Fitted with stones from Germany, the unique wirework was formed, then plated. 6". Courtesy of Diane S. Hobé. Rare.

Cast-silver frames from the 1800s to the early part of the 1900s were manufactured in extremely ornate designs. Often marked 800 (silver), sterling, or 925, these frames feature intricate scenes that include winged dragons, cherubs, animals, gargoyles, horse drawn chariots, Medusa, and a host of other fascinating subjects. The American Gorham Manufacturing Company and the Italian-based Coppini Silversmiths are two companies that struck their marks on similarly handsome frames. The famous Tiffany Company also made frames of gold and silver at that time.

The designing of vintage purse frames was an art form unto itself, evident from early drawings by the E.A. Bliss Company. For a few short years beginning in 1911, exceptional designs for purses and purse frames were created with intent for production. Sketched, then colored on special wax paper, these originals incorporated gemstones, enameling, and innovative shapes. Often the paper was folded in half, with one side purposely having a slight variation in the design, either through

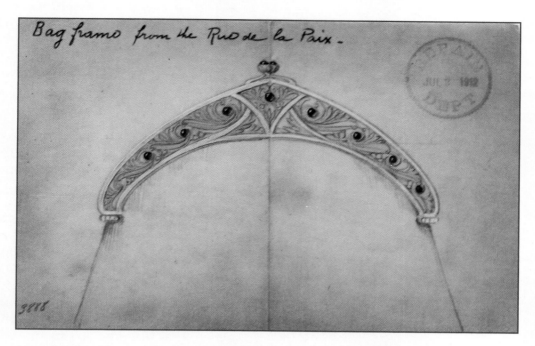

An example of how a vintage purse frame is designed. First sketched in pencil, it is then tipped in color on special waxed paper. This one was conceived by the Bliss Company, 1912. Courtesy of the Napier Company archives, photograph by Walter Kitik.

Faux jewels arrived in the United States in folded paper packets with tissue inserts. Sold by the gross, they were available in a variety of shapes and colors. Those with polished, domed tops are called cabochons, while faceted stones are identified by shape, such as roundel, baguette, oval, etc. Measured in millimeters, certain glass jewels have foil on their undersides. This special finishing process allows more light to be reflected through the sparkling faux gemstone. Shown are stones from Czechoslovakia with a packet from France. The Curiosity Shop. NPA.

choice of color or with the stones selected. Utilizing these sketches, the company intended to produce a line of high quality frames and purses. Some of the frames were to be cast from a mold, while others were to be stamped out on large presses. Many contained various penciled notations in French or English. A few designs showed dimensions and pinpointed various parts that needed added illustration to clarify the design. Occasionally, there were other sketches on the same page displaying the bag from a different angle.

It is not known whether these unique pieces of artwork were drawn by the famed Tiffany apprentice, William Rettenmeyer, who was employed by Bliss during this time. In 1913, Rettenmeyer retired as head of the design department and his son Frederick took over his responsibilities. The Napier Company, as it became known later, was closed in 1999.

The Whiting and Davis Company produced over 1200 frame variations throughout their history of purse manufacturing. Many of them proved to be quite successful. One, in particular, had a smooth rigid metal handle instead of the usual

An intricate design for a cast frame using cabochons. Courtesy of the Napier Company archives, photograph by Walter Kitik.

linked carry chain. This was not well received by the public. Customers favored metal linked carry chains over rigid metal handles by a ratio of nearly 500 to 1. Consequently, this gave the rigid handled purse a short production life and those possessing this feature are few and highly collectible.

The Hobé Company made especially beautiful, opulent jeweled frames with an unmatched blend of gilded metal work and lavish imported German stones. Jacques Hobé conceptualized his business in Paris in the year 1887. He started with the manufacture of fine jewelry at affordable prices for those of middle class status. Now, more than a century later, the innovations of Jacques Hobé are legendary.

His son, William, relocated to the United States in 1915. Soon afterward, Hollywood stars and producers began seeking his unique creations. Demand for his work increased, and before long he opened a store on Rodeo Drive in Beverly Hills, California.

His sons, Robert and Donald, were also designers and continued William's work. Their use of stones and beads obtained from around the world included gemstones such as jade, tiger eye, lapis lazuli, turquoise, malachite, and assorted agates. The brothers became renowned experts in fine jade selection and in choosing high quality imita-

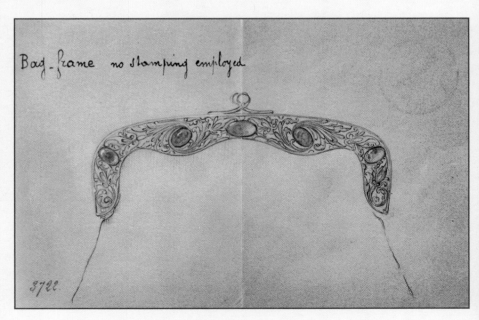

Bag-frame no stamping employed

3722

tion pearls from the island of Majorca. They developed a special finish called Formula 70, consisting of 22 karat electrolytic gold, and they continued to bring fresh and innovative designs to the public, as did their father and grandfather before them.

Beginning in the 1930s, the Hobé Company designed many wonderful purse frames. After each frame was drawn and production begun, bezel settings were formed in sterling silver. Before being set with stones imported from Germany, intricate wirework was added, then the plating process began. One of their distinctive frame designs consists of chunky glass jeweled hearts, placed in embellished metal settings surrounded by other stones. Appraised in 1993 by Don S. Hobé, he described the frame as having "clear cut chatons (without foil) and each stone is set in a milligrained bezel." He dates the piece between 1929 to 1934 and establishes value in the range of $2950.00 to $3450.00. Their infamous blend of gilded metal work with a variety of lavish, unfoiled stones sets their work apart. Occasionally they incorporated carved ivory, cinnabar, and other unorthodox materials to add a dramatic flair. James William Hobé, grandson of William Hobé, continues to design today.

A stunning 1920s vintage purse frame with stones, matched with a new crocheted purse pouch. Courtesy of Marilyn Pivnick Purses, photograph by Lisa Statt. $600.00 – 800.00.

A distinctive Hobé frame design consisting of chunky glass jeweled hearts, placed in embellished metal settings and surrounded by other stones. Don S. Hobé, appraising the frame in 1993, described it as having "clear cut chatons" (without foil) which are "set in a milligrained bezel." He dated the piece between 1929 and 1934 and established its value between $2,950.00 and $3,450.00. A sewn in label in the lining states: "By Hobé." 9½ x 9½. Author's collection. Very rare.

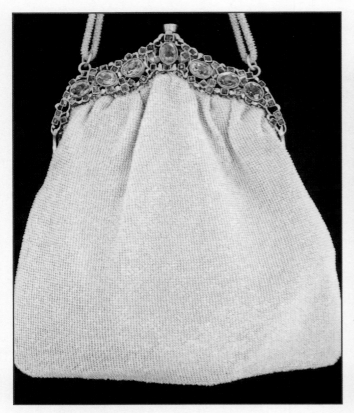

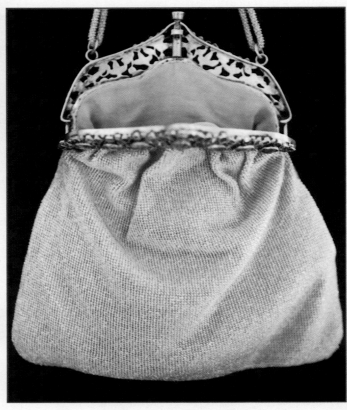

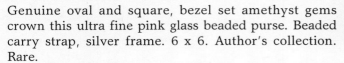

Genuine oval and square, bezel set amethyst gems crown this ultra fine pink glass beaded purse. Beaded carry strap, silver frame. 6 x 6. Author's collection. Rare.

Out of over 1200 frame variations throughout their history of purse manufacturing, the Whiting and Davis Company produced one type with a smooth rigid metal handle instead of the usual linked carry chain. However, customers favored metal linked carry chains over rigid metal handles by a ratio of nearly 500 to 1. Consequently, this gave the rigid handled purse a short production life and those possessing this feature are few and highly collectible. 5 x 6. The Curiosity Shop. $175.00 – 275.00.

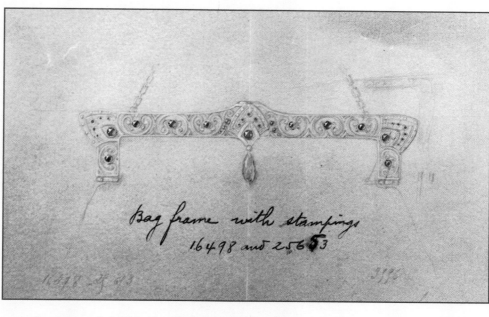

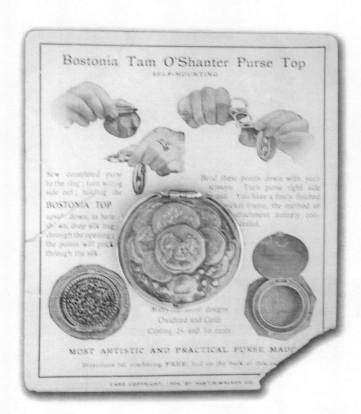

A Bostonia Tam O'Shanter purse frame is mounted on an advertisement with instructions for its use. The Curiosity Shop. $75.00 – 125.00.

Sterling Silver figural purse frame with an intricate scene that includes animals and winged dragons. 7 x 10. The Curiosity Shop. $250.00 – 350.00.

A signed embossed Tiffany 14K gold frame sets off this fine glass beaded floral purse beautifully. 8 x 10. Author's collection. Rare.

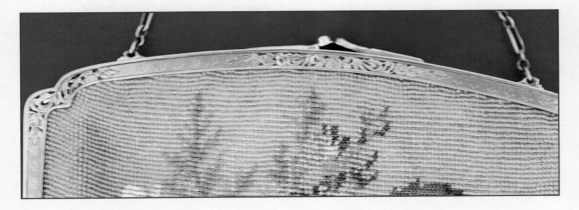

A new black crocheted pouch is a perfect contrast to the green jeweled marcasite frame from the 1920s. 6 x 7. Courtesy of Marilyn Pivnick Purses, photograph by Lisa Statt. $600.00 – 800.00.

Carnelian and marcasite bejeweled purse frame from the 1920s paired with a new crocheted pouch. 6½ x 7. Courtesy of Marilyn Pivnick Purses, photograph by Lisa Statt. $600.00 – 800.00.

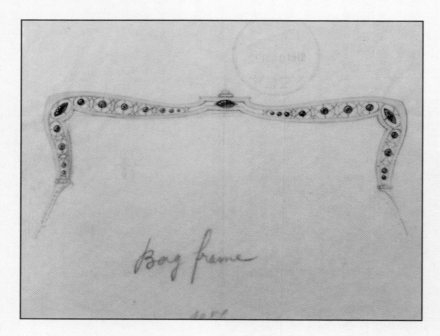

Courtesy of the Napier Company archives, photograph by Walter Kitik.

Arched shaped frame in a unique scalloped design set with mottled green cabochons and a variety of bezel set jewels. 6". Author's collection. $500.00 – 700.00.

Original design drawing for a 1913 frame. Notice the wide carry strap and sketched side view version to the left. Courtesy of the Napier Company archives, photograph by Walter Kitik.

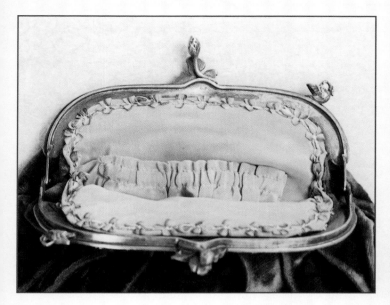

This ornate silver cherub motif frame, shown open, was cast between 1890 – 1910. The 800 silver mark impressed upon the frame's interior is barely visible under the cherub decorated thumb clasp. Arched swans' heads accommodate the carry chain while the interior reveals a beige silk lining complete with floral trim. 6½ x 8. The Curiosity Shop. $295.00 – 395.00.

Blue teardrops with crystal sets embellish this intricate metal worked Hobé purse frame. Stones were imported from Germany. 1930. 7". Author's collection. Rare.

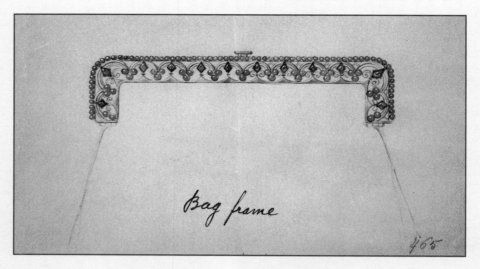

Bliss Company's design drawing. Tiny purple stones in a cluster formation resemble grapes. Courtesy of the Napier Company archives, photograph by Walter Kitik.

Two Hobé frames. 6". The Curiosity Shop. $350.00 – 650.00.

Horse drawn chariot motif silver frame. 2 w x 6. Author's collection. $350.00 – 450.00.

European black velvet bag with 800 silver frame. Dual acorn designed clasp. Circa 1890 – 1910. 7½ x 8. From the collection of Paula Higgins. $295.00 – 395.00.

Multicolored crystal jeweled Hobé frame with black pouch. Made in New York with stones imported from Germany. Circa 1930 – 40. 7 x 6. Courtesy of Diane S. Hobé. Rare.

Cherubs were popular designs on ornate silver frames from this period, often depicted dancing, plucking fruit, or playing musical instruments. Silver frame on velvet pouch. Circa 1890 – 1910. 6½ x 8. The Curiosity Shop. $395.00 – 495.00.

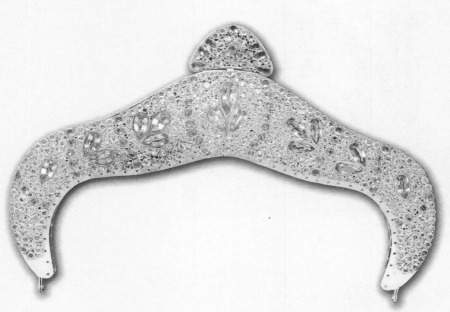

The largest known Hobe purse frame. The unique blend of gilded metal work and varied lavish unfoiled stones sets their work apart. 12". Courtesy of Diane S. Hobé. Very rare.

Red and green bezel set cabochons adorn this ornate plunger top frame. Detail includes a pair of swan carry chain connectors. 7½". The Curiosity Shop. $450.00 – 650.00.

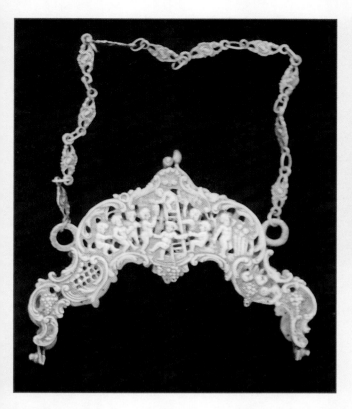

Early twentieth century purse frame designed to be enameled in white on gold. Courtesy of the Napier Company archives, photograph by Walter Kitik.

Elaborate silver frame features cherubs on a ladder plucking grapes. Ornate carry chain. 6". Signed Coppini. The Curiosity Shop. $395.00 – 495.00.

One-of-a-kind 14k and sterling silver floral topped clutch bag with bezel sets featuring a hand-carved ivory central medallion. 8 x 13. Courtesy of Diane S. Hobé. Rare.

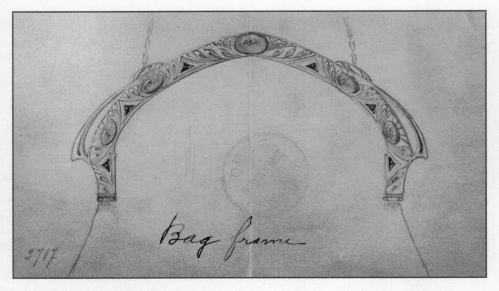

Oval cabochons adorn this Art Nouveau motif frame design. 1912. Courtesy of the Napier Company archives, photograph by Walter Kitik.

A wide ornate cherub motif frame is paired with a new white crocheted pouch. 6 x 7. Courtesy of Marilyn Pivnick Purses, photograph by Lisa Statt. $600.00 – 800.00.

Well crafted Hobé frame incorporates tiny colored stones to form flowers. 6". Courtesy of Diane S. Hobé. Rare.

An unmarked cast frame. 7". The Curiosity Shop. $295.00 – 395.00.

Ornate cast silver winged cherub motif purse frame with an elaborate chatelaine hook. 7 x 10. From the collection of Paula Higgins. $395.00 – 495.00.

A wide jeweled frame is encrusted with an assortment of cabochon and faceted stones. 2w x 7. Author's collection. $595.00 – 750.00.

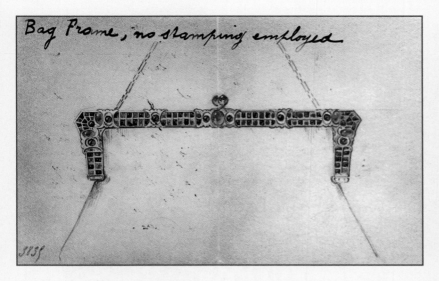

Courtesy of the Napier Company archives, photograph by Walter Kitik.

A velvet flower basket motif purse body complements this jeweled frame. 6 x 9. The Curiosity Shop. $400.00 – 550.00.

Extra fancy wide jewel encrusted frame from the early twentieth century. 1½ w x 6″ Author's collection. $700.00 – 900.00.

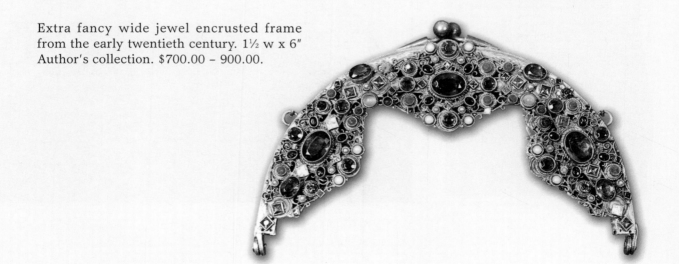

Floral motif silver colored frame. 6".
The Curiosity Shop, photograph by
Irene Clarke. $150.00 – 250.00.

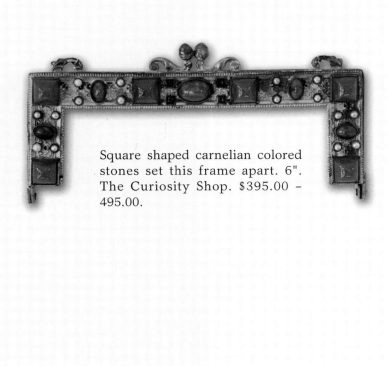

Square shaped carnelian colored
stones set this frame apart. 6".
The Curiosity Shop. $395.00 –
495.00.

The eager little souls in these old photographs discovered early in their lives the joy of owning a special purse. Notice their little hands gingerly clutching their prized possessions. Behold their proud, wide eyes as they make efforts to still themselves for the camera. One can just imagine their enthusiasm when summoned for the photo. "But wait, Papa! I must get my purse!" called over a shoulder as delicate footsteps quickly made their way toward a hiding place that held the coveted accessory.

Children's purses of the early twentieth century often pictured a popular cartoon type of character. Some of the illustrious ones are easily identifiable, while others, including those that were fleetingly faddish or created on the purse maker's whim, are nearly impossible to identify. In either case, there is a distinct charm and great challenge in collecting children's purses, even though some were originally sold inexpensively. Children's bags were generally well used and played with and, as a consequence, were not always treated with optimum care. Those that were not discarded or lost altogether over the years might be found in disrepair, if one is fortunate enough to encounter them at all.

In 1924, a mini Delysia vanity bag by Whiting and Davis, called The Baby Peggy was introduced. An advertisement for the purse reads: "for her daughter, in gold, silver, or colored enameled with silken top." This was a brilliant strategic campaign as it emphasized that smaller matching versions of the Delysia could be affordably purchased for young girls. The Whiting and Davis Company was notorious for extensive advertising in popular publications. They were especially cognizant to campaign heavily during the holidays with an obvious slant toward gift giving.

Glass beaded purses created for children might have the image of a train, an animal, or other subjects that children hold dear. In small sizes to accommodate tiny hands, some of these petite gems were fashioned by devoted family members, while others could be purchased at retail outlets.

An unknown celluloid manufacturer created a series of colorful coin purses, each depicting a different subject, mainly consisting of animals. Dogs, pigs, cats, and bunnies decorate these little charmers, while adjustable cords for tiny wrists were provided. This series also included a witch. The round lids, often in a contrasting color, slid up on the cord for access into the tiny receptacle. One can just imagine the resounding "click" that pennies must have made as they hit the hard celluloid at the bottom of the purse!

A purse is featured in this advertisement for thread stating, "Lucy Locket, lost her pocket, Kitty Fisher found it; There was not a penny in it, But a ribbon round it."

Chatelaine purses that attach to a hook worn on the waist are often considered an accessory enjoyed by adult women. However, in some affluent families, there is photographic evidence that children, too, benefited from the "hands free" convenience of the chatelaine purse.

In the 1920s, figural felt doll purses were created. These fascinating bags have a snap in the back that provides access to the interior and includes a felt strap for carrying. Complete with cut out legs and arms, this dual personality purse/toy was a favorite among children. It was either sold inexpensively or gifted to potential customers, as evidenced by a product endorsement, which is occasionally discovered on the back of the doll's head.

Whiting and Davis created several Mickey and Minnie Mouse mesh purses in the 1930s. These famous Disney cartoon characters were incorporated into the bag in several different ways: the couple embossed into a colorful frame; one appearing as a metal cutout dangling freely from the frame; or Mickey Mouse enameled onto the body of a flat enameled mesh purse. The company also manufactured a small mesh purse that depicts the Three Little Pigs in the form of a stamped metal cutout hanging from the frame.

Regardless of who made them or how economical they might have been, one thing is known for certain: when a child posed for a photo with her purse held proudly in the forefront, she most certainly wished for the world to see it!

This happy little girl clutches a child's purse with a character depicted on the front. Children's purses often pictured a famous or faddish cartoon-type character that was popular at that time. Proudly holding the purse in the forefront, she most certainly wished for the world to see it.

Twins with similar tastes both share their love of flowers and purses.

A fabric purse with a silk-trimmed painted cartoon style face affixed to its front. Circa 1920s. 4½ x 4½. The Curiosity Shop. $200.00 – 300.00.

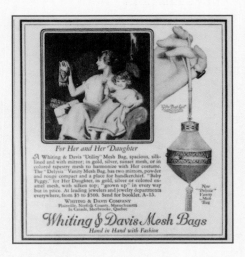

"For her and her daughter." The Delysia and the Baby Peggy are depicted in a 1920s advertisement showing a happy holiday scene of mother and daughter opening gifts manufactured by the Whiting and Davis Company. *Cosmopolitan*, December, 1924.

A brilliant strategic campaign by the Whiting and Davis company was to advertise affordable purses "for her daughter."

From the hat to the gloves she is quite fancily dressed. Of course, she could not forget her purse!

A mini Delysia vanity bag by Whiting and Davis called The Baby Peggy. An advertisement dated 1924 reads, "for her daughter, in gold, silver, or colored enameled with silken top." 3 x 5. From the collection of Elaine Lehn. $800.00 – 1,000.00.

Nicely detailed glass beaded floral purse with a simple frame. Beaded purses of this size might have the image of a train, an animal, or other objects that children hold dear. 3 x 3. The Curiosity Shop. $75.00 – 125.00.

Two little girls, two little purses. This photo was taken just after the turn of the century.

This card entitled "Blue Bloods," indicates that, even when a lady is helping with a horse show, she still remembers to carry her bag.

This early twentieth-century pair, most likely brother and sister, are all dressed up and ready to attend an important event.

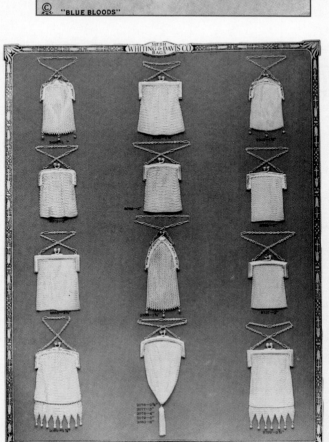

From the catalog entitled "Whiting and Davis Mesh Bags," 1922. Courtesy of the Napier Company archives, photograph by Walter Kitik.

Time to enjoy Easter with an oversized bonnet and a pretty little reticule. Circa 1916.

Charming beaded figural purse depicting a terrier type dog. Some mini beaded purses depicted animals and subjects of interest to children. 3 x 3. The Curiosity Shop. $125.00 – 175.00.

The lady in the coffee advertisement proudly carries a purse. This card was one of a series.

A Connecticut photograph taken shortly after the turn of the century.

Charming celluloid coin purses, each depicting a different animal subject. Here, a dog, pig, and a bunny. This series also included a cat and a witch. Adjustable cords for tiny wrists. 2 x 2. The Curiosity Shop. $95.00 – 135.00.

Tea advertisement from the Great Atlantic and Pacific Tea Company (A&P). Note the early reticule carried by the woman. Circa 1882.

Early plastic adjustable wrist cord puppy purse. Those large wistful eyes beg, "Take me home!" 3½ x 3½. The Curiosity Shop. $65.00 – 95.00.

Who let the cat out of the bag?

Notice how the purse style changed on this card from 1940.

A photograph shows a pair of twin sisters wearing lovely chatelaine purses that attach to a hook worn on the waist. Often considered an accessory enjoyed by adult women, here, evidence that affluent children benefited from this "hands free" convenience. Boston, Massachusetts.

The family relates that this lovely beaded purse was given to this darling baby to keep her interest while the picture was taken. Courtesy of Fern Dengis.

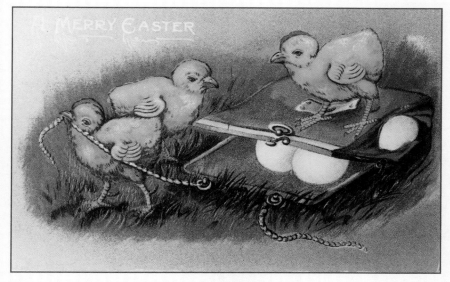

1909.

1912.

Dressed in character for a play, the outfits were complete with purses.

Felt doll purses from the 1920s could vary slightly in color combinations and styles. Those with advertisements were either sold inexpensively or gifted to potential customers as they occasionally carried a product endorsement appearing on the back of the doll's head. An advertisement for a shoe shop is revealed on the back of the brown doll. 5 x 7. Author's collection. $200.00 – 350.00.

Illinois.

Velvet purse/doll combination with applied felt flowers. A painted face, wig, and felt hands complete the doll, while the purse portion has a carry strap and a zipper in the back. 5 x 7. Author's collection. $200.00 – 375.00.

1920s felt doll purse. This dual personality purse/toy has a snap in the back that provides access to the interior. It also includes a matching strap for carrying. 5 x 7. Author's collection. $200.00 – 350.00.

Whiting and Davis Mickey and Minnie Mouse framed ring mesh purse. 1930s. 3¾ x 3. From the collection of Paula Higgins. $500.00 – 650.00.

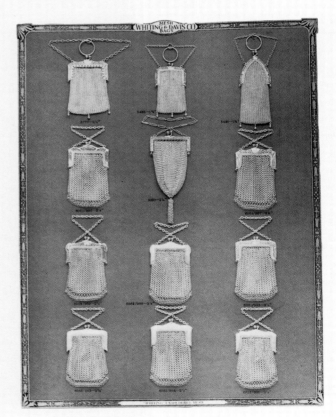

From the catalog entitled "Whiting and Davis Mesh Bags," 1922. Courtesy of the Napier Company archives, photograph by Walter Kitik.

Celluloid purses and frames encompass themes spanning from the romantic to the macabre. Some extreme examples feature a depiction of Satan against a scaly background joined with a black jet embellished mourning pouch, heraldic beasts with protruding tongues atop a curiously patterned velvet purse, and a fierce lion with exaggerated whiskers peering through green tropical brush.

Romantic themes cover everything from roses on a garden trellis, as well as swans and doves with deeply carved feathers, to a variety of flowers such as lily of the valley and lotus blossoms. Fleur de lis and basket weaves, acorns and leaves, foliage, cattails, and even cameos adorn these celluloid creations.

The surreal, too, is exemplified in the fairy-tale-type figure of a Geisha's head on a translucent winged dragonfly embodying the art nouveau movement. A noteworthy art deco suede purse with a finely carved celluloid panel features a different fairytale like figure — a nude atop what looks like a large leaf. Upon closer inspection, however, a curious long legged bird comes into focus. One more depicts a human infant that seems to hatch from a cracking egg. Still another portrays the stuff that makes for many a good fable — a long tailed snarling dragon.

The animal kingdom is also represented. Greyhounds float to the finish line and stylized seahorses flaunt curly tails and extended tongues. A menagerie of rodents, cats, dragonflies, armadillos, rams, and elephants (with trunks lifted for good luck) adorn some of the many diverse celluloid purse frames.

Somewhat bizarre figures such as a Buddhist, a Mongolian, Harlequin, and a pair of Chinamen with their hair and mustaches entwined, have found their places among premier collections of celluloid. A discus thrower forever holds his pose on an uncommon purse frame while details of the vintage clothing the athlete wears give clues to dating the piece. Could it be a rare scene from a historic Olympic event?

An important piece of literary artwork taken from the macabre genius of Edgar Allen Poe's *The Raven* is depicted on an exceptional celluloid frame. Poe's brooding work is fraught with mystery and foreboding as he describes the disturbing visit from a raven tapping on his window lattice. The

Remarkable Satan motif celluloid frame mourning purse. A scaly snakelike texture decorates the background — evidence of the painstaking detail of this piece of artwork. Beautifully executed in color with ivy leaves, the demonic figure appears on both sides. 4¾ x 5. Author's collection, photograph by Irene Clarke. Very rare.

This black grosgrain purse has an appliqué panel of jet beads embellishing the front. Lightweight, the polished black jet made from coal was considered suitable mourning décor. 8 x 12.

Edgar Allen Poe's 1845 poem, *The Raven*, is depicted on an exceptional celluloid frame. The brooding written work is fraught with mystery as Poe describes the disturbing visit from a raven tapping on his window lattice. The blackness of the background on the frame conveys Poe's sentiment, "Deep into that darkness peering..." Icicles pictured throughout the frame indicate "bleak December," while the black raven is "perched above my chamber door." 4¾. Author's collection, photograph by Irene Clarke. Rare.

---

blackness of the background on the frame illustrates Poe's vision, "Deep into that darkness peering..." Icicles pictured throughout the frame indicate a "bleak December," while the black raven is "perched above my chamber door," from the poem of 1845.

Interest in things Egyptian was re-ignited with the discovery of King Tutankhamun's tomb in the 1920s. Drumbeats of ancient Egypt must have beckoned purse frame artisans too, as images of lotus blossoms, sacred cats with human heads, Egyptian handmaidens, Pharaohs, and the like were immortalized in celluloid.

Before celluloid was invented providing all of us with these wonderful figurals, a technological race to find an alternative source for making purse frames, ornamental jewelry, and other items ensued. One of the materials in use prior to the invention of celluloid was tortoise shell, a natural plastic derived from the hawksbill turtle. It could be heated and molded, then shaped or cut into many forms. There was also a need to find a substitute for ivory, amber (fossilized resin), and coral. At the time, ivory, which was derived from elephant tusks, had been rounded into billiard balls and carved into other items, including intricately carved purse frames. Obviously, these sources were limited and scarce. If they were available, they were quite expensive.

The solution came in 1869 from John W. Hyatt of Albany, New York. His relentless experimenting with reducing pyroxylin solutions resulted in the discovery of celluloid. The invention of this synthetic plastic marked the beginning of the celluloid industry.

Lightweight and moldable, it could be used for making a vast assortment of objects: purses, hair combs and brushes, dominos, amber pipe bits, fancy boxes, collars, dolls, poker dice, dress stays, jewelry — the list of novelty items is virtually limitless.

A fierce lion with exaggerated whiskers peers through green tropical brush. Dark glass beaded body, celluloid link chain handle. 5½ x 9. From the collection of Diane Goldfarb. $700.00 – 900.00.

Because it could be manufactured to resemble natural ivory and tortoise shell, celluloid looked more expensive than it actually was. Purse frames with irregular brown stripes that resemble expensive tortoise shell and cream-colored frames that look remarkably like ivory could now be produced in quantity. By 1896, celluloid objects such as pin trays, hair combs, fancy trinkets, and other vanity items could be purchased for between twenty-five cents to one dollar.

The basis of celluloid: cotton, has the chemical name, cellulose. After being separated from certain substances that make it hard, it could be processed into celluloid. The manufacturing process was lengthy and required at least 20 distinct operations. One of these operations involved the addition of camphor. Another was to add sulphur, the basis of sulphuric acid.

These ingredients were ground in a mill, pressed into cakes, and thoroughly dried. Alcohol, then pigments and dyes were added to the dough-like mass. Without these ingredients, celluloid would resemble gelatin or transparent horn in its original state. It was then manufactured in sheets, rods, and tubes.

Rough sheets or slabs formed on rolls were placed in large iron molds and solidified by heat and hydraulic pressure. Sheets of various thicknesses were planed from the blocks. They were dyed, seasoned, and polished.

The novelty and specialty department was operated by experts and jewelers who applied their own artistic flare. Glass jewels could be pressed into a celluloid purse front for added sparkle, and later, a silk tassel could finish the piece with a touch of drama. Hair combs, brooches, and necklaces were set with rhinestones for added glamour.

Despite the wonders of celluloid, there was a grave risk involved in its production. It was not long before this early plastic was determined to be unsafe because of its high degree of flammability. The original Newark, New Jersey, factory was mysteriously destroyed by fire in 1875, just a short time after celluloid was invented. Although the factory was quickly relocated to continue production of celluloid, its flammable tendency could not be denied. Documents from as early as 1910 required that drying furnaces not be allowed to exceed 113 degrees for fear of explosions.

In time, safer plastic substitutes were developed and the manufacture of celluloid was discontinued. In 1934 it was banned from the market by federal law. The purses and frames produced prior to the ban, however, have steadily increased in value over the years because of the relatively short production life, therefore, the limited supply, of these celluloid treasures.

Heraldic beasts with protruding tongues embellish a brown-toned cream celluloid frame. Curiously patterned velvet pouch with matching carry cord. 5½ x 8. Author's collection, photograph by Irene Clarke. $800.00 – 1,000.00.

A colored rose motif celluloid frame is designed to emulate toned old ivory on the façade and tortoiseshell along the top. Floral grosgrain pouch with matching handle. 5¼ x 8. Author's collection, photograph by Irene Clarke. $700.00 – 900.00.

Lightweight and moldable, celluloid could be used for making many types of objects, including purse frames, as shown in this photo taken in the 1920s.

Shown open to reveal a blue silk lining with frilled edge, pocket, and covered mirror.

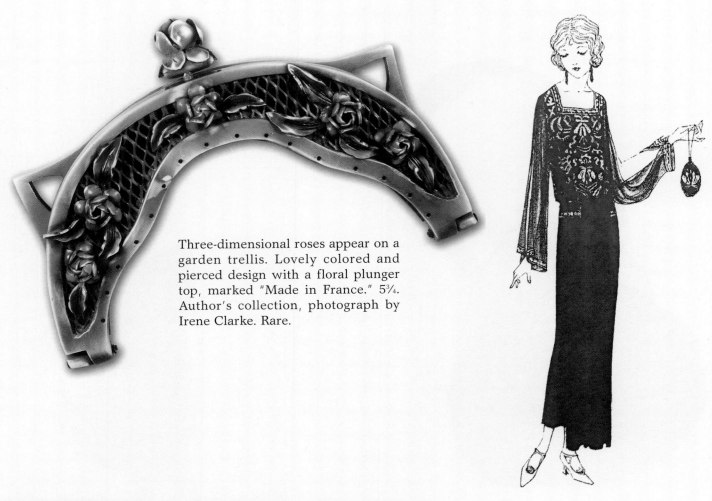

Three-dimensional roses appear on a garden trellis. Lovely colored and pierced design with a floral plunger top, marked "Made in France." 5¾. Author's collection, photograph by Irene Clarke. Rare.

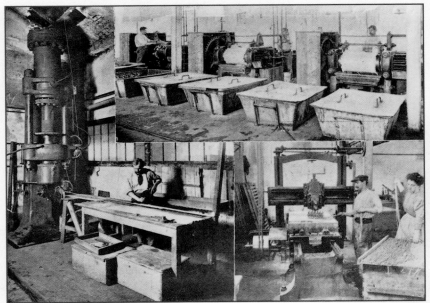

The process of manufacturing celluloid required at least twenty distinct operations. Here workers are drawing tubes of celluloid, rolling sheets of it, and cutting out rods. *Scientific American*, 1910.

Painted floral motif purse with matching flowered celluloid frame. Pull over clasp. 5 x 7. The Curiosity Shop. $500.00 – 650.00.

Dual colored Egyptian motif with an ivory colored figure. The color red is dominant on the edges and continues to the interior of frame. The plunger top is shaped like an Egyptian headdress in red. Plain black silk pouch. 5¾ x 7. Author's collection, photograph by Irene Clarke. Rare.

Ivory colored rose frame shown slightly open. Brown silk pouch. Notice the detail in the leaves. 4½ x 6. From the collection of Diane Goldfarb. Rare.

Large celluloid red rose with a clasp entirely disguised as foliage. Black silk body. 5 x 8. From the collection of Diane Goldfarb. Rare.

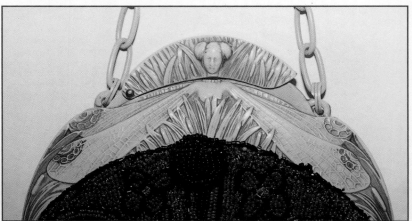

The surreal is exemplified in the figure of a Geisha head with a translucent winged dragonfly body in a striking art nouveau design. A glass beaded purse in a highly stylized floral motif with triple loop fringe encircling the entire bag body. 10 x 8½. From the collection of Paula Higgins. $800.00 – 1,200.00.

A dragonfly Geisha girl in color. Details such as wing texture and cattails are shown. Marked "Made in France." 5½. Author's collection, photograph by Irene Clarke. $800.00 – 1,000.00.

Unusual art deco suede purse with a finely carved celluloid panel in shallow relief featuring a fairytale type nude atop what looks like a large leaf. Instead, on closer inspection, a curious long legged bird becomes evident. It has thin silver embossed trim border, with a three sectional silk interior, the center division of which is a change purse lined in kid. French, 1920s. 5½ x 6½. Author's collection. Rare.

Stunning celluloid colored frame combined with a new purse body. 6½ x 8. Courtesy of Marilyn Pivnick Purses, photograph by Lisa Statt. $700.00 – 900.00.

Celluloid frame with a colored swan scene. 4¾. Author's collection, photograph by Irene Clarke. Rare.

A black dragonfly and floral fretted pierced designed purse frame is combined with a silk floral pouch. 5¼ x 9. Author's collection, photograph by Irene Clarke. $650.00 – 850.00.

An armadillo figural celluloid purse frame accompanied by a glass beaded, colorful, stylized floral design body. 7 x 11. From the collection of Diane Goldfarb. $800.00 – 1,000.00.

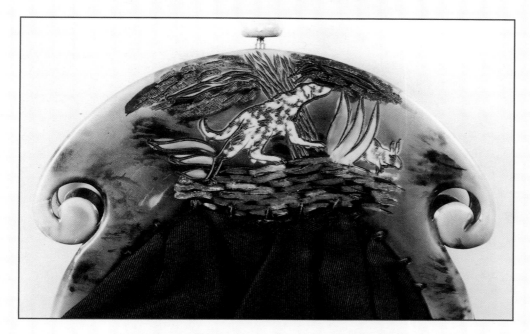

Carved hunting scene of a dog chasing a hare through foliage. On the reverse, lily of the valley. A curled design enhances the frame's sides. Contains a plunger top and black grosgrain pouch. 5¼ x 7. Author's collection, photograph by Irene Clarke. $800.00 – 1,000.00.

A greyhound floating to the finish line serves as an ornamental handle on this figural celluloid purse frame. New black crocheted pouch. Courtesy of Marilyn Pivnick Purses, photograph by Lisa Statt. $1,000.00 – 1,200.00.

Butterscotch Bakelite crouching wolf purse handle. Bakelite is a phenolic plastic used in the early twentieth century. 8¼. Author's collection, photograph by Irene Clarke. Rare.

Ivory colored semicircle surmounted by a pair of stylized seahorses flaunting curly tails and extended tongues. Crocheted pouch. 5¾. The Curiosity Shop, photograph by Irene Clarke. $600.00 – 800.00.

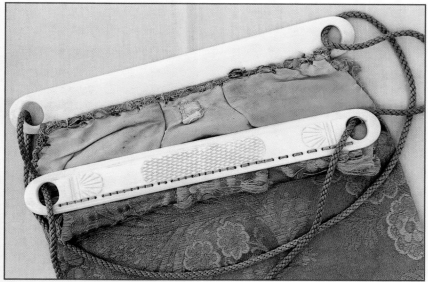

Two ivory bars with carved patterns form the side frames of this bag along with a pouch of faded brocade. 7 x 7. The Curiosity Shop, photograph by Irene Clarke. $275.00 – 395.00.

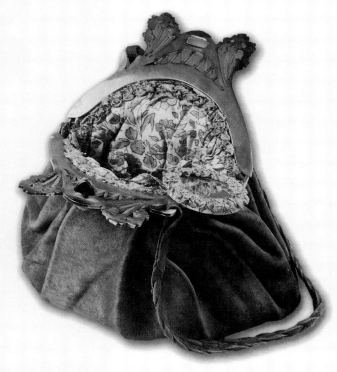

Latticed celluloid frame with unusual foliage surmounts this suede purse. Red thumb clasp knob, plaited suede carry handle. 5½ x 8. Author's collection, photograph by Irene Clarke. $800.00 – 1,000.00.

A cotton floral interior with pocket, covered mirror, and a frilled edge is visible when opened.

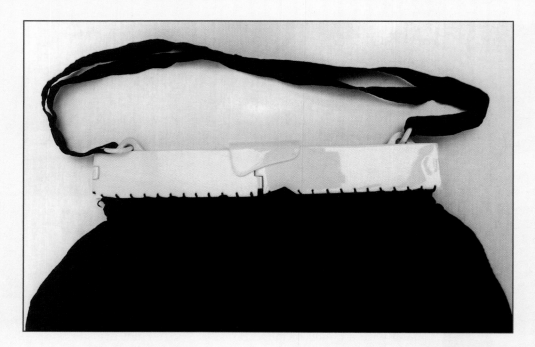

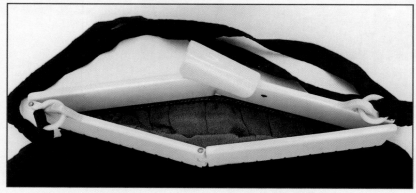

Ivory colored celluloid frame opens to a square to allow access to the purse. Black silk pouch. 8½ x 7. The Curiosity Shop, photograph by Irene Clarke. $200.00 – 300.00.

Wide arched floral motif in tan and ivory colored celluloid. 4½. Author's collection, photograph by Irene Clarke. $700.00 – 900.00.

A discus thrower forever holds his pose on a rare purse frame. The athlete's vintage clothing provides a clue for dating the piece. Beige silk crochet pouch with fringe. The interior reveals a silk lining. 5½ x 10. Author's collection, photograph by Irene Clarke. Very rare.

A simple triple floral design with twisted rope pattern. Lovely blue velvet floral pouch. 6¼ x 7. Author's collection, photograph by Irene Clarke. $600.00 – 800.00.

Striking floral frame and purse combination. A colored carved celluloid frame is paired with an ornate silk stitched floral outlined by French cut steel beads. Generous fringe. 5½ x 10. From the collection of Diane Goldfarb. $1,000.00 – 1,200.00.

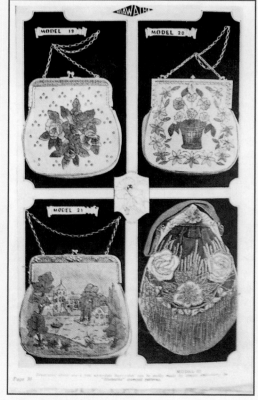

Purses that were made by embroidery on Hiawatha stamped patterns. The example on the bottom right depicts a popular pattern often combined with a celluloid frame. A *Distinctive Group of Beaded Bags*, 1925.

The same style of bag with a slightly different artist's interpretation. 5½ x 7½. The Curiosity Shop. $1,000.00 – 1,200.00.

Pierced design of acorns and leaves in toned celluloid. Bronze silk crochet pouch with deep fringe, and orange cotton lining with braid trim finish. 6¾ x 12. Author's collection, photograph by Irene Clarke. $600.00 – 800.00.

Flared openwork designed celluloid frame, plunger top. Pretty newer crocheted pouch with plaited carry handle. 5½ x 7. Courtesy of Marilyn Pivnick Purses, photograph by Lisa Statt. $700.00 – 900.00.

Honey colored celluloid open worked frame. Brown satin pouch with flock velvet pattern. 7 x 8. Author's collection, photograph by Irene Clarke. $600.00 – 800.00.

Stunning floral flip-top catch frame with color that matches the toned floral cotton pouch in a striking fashion. 5½ x 9. Author's collection, photograph by Irene Clarke. $700.00 – 900.00.

Silk floral lining with yellow rose braid edging.

Celluloid was manufactured to resemble natural tortoise shell, evident with this purse frame. Black silk pouch with tab and plunger top. 3¼ x 4. The Curiosity Shop, photograph by Irene Clarke. $300.00 – 400.00.

Bending celluloid hairpins in the factory. As early as 1910, celluloid drying furnaces were not allowed to exceed 113 degrees for fear of explosion. *Scientific American.*

Silk lining with red braid trim to match exterior piping.

Brightly colored cherry purse frame and a green cloth pouch trimmed with red piping. 5½ x 9. Author's collection, photograph by Irene Clarke. Rare.

Made entirely of celluloid rings, this unusual lightweight purse has a diamond shaped, tortoise colored lid with applied flowers. The lid lifts and slides along the beaded carry handle for interior access. It is difficult to find these in excellent condition. 4½ x 8. The Curiosity Shop. Rare.

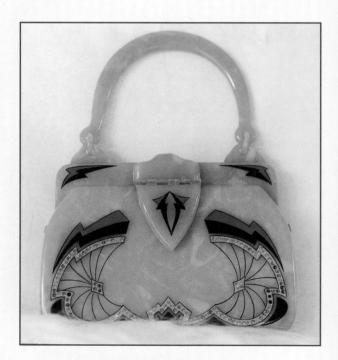

Black celluloid semicircle covered on both sides in diamanté with an art deco flare. Silk pouch and carry handle. 4½ x 8. The Curiosity Shop, photograph by Irene Clarke. $350.00 – 450.00.

Art deco all-celluloid purse, embedded with glass stones and painted for effect. Rigid handle, over clasp. 5½ x 7. The Curiosity Shop. $800.00 – 1,000.00.

Diamanté leaf design on a black celluloid frame. 6¼. The Curiosity Shop, photograph by Irene Clarke. $350.00 – 450.00.

Chinamen face each other, their hair and mustaches entwined. Colorful and unusual celluloid frame, new pouch. 4½ x 6½. Courtesy of Marilyn Pivnick Purses, photograph by Lisa Statt. $1,200.00.

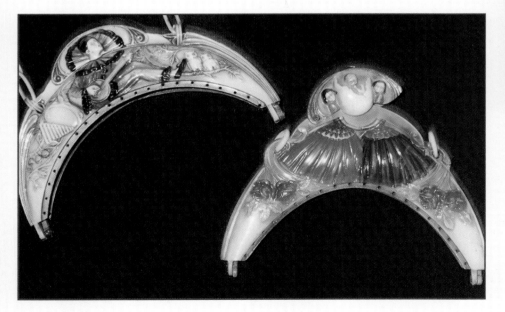

Two extra fancy colored figural celluloid frames. One depicts Harlequin; the other, a fairytale type scene of two women and a baby that seems to hatch from a cracking egg. Notice that the baby is on the overclasp of the frame, shown slightly open here. 5¾, 5½. Author's collection. Rare.

This purse was reputedly owned by Lily Chaplin, an early twentieth century dancer whose last performance was in Berlin in 1918. This swansdown feather covered domed frame is a striking contrast to the black crocheted pouch interspersed with sparkling cut glass beads. 4 x 6. Author's collection, Photograph by Irene Clarke. Rare.

"Colibris Brevete" is signed in gold on the interior of the celluloid frame, along with "Made in France," and a seahorse design. Colibri translates to hummingbird, brevet to patent. Black cotton lining.

Oriental theme celluloid figural frame in ivory color. New crocheted pouch. 5½ x 7. Courtesy of Marilyn Pivnick Purses, photograph by Lisa Statt. $700.00 – 900.00.

Left: Bulbous egg-shaped striped celluloid purse with carry cord and silk tassel in a red and black color combination. The interior holds a pretty linen lined pocket with floral braid trim. 3½ x 5. The Curiosity Shop. $600.00 – 800.00.

Right: Matching striped black and cream celluloid dance purse. Rhinestones decorate the top and bottom knobs with accessibility via thumb knobs at the center of the purse. 3½ x 5. The Curiosity Shop. $600.00 – 800.00.

Celluloid dance purses with tassels were manufactured in a variety of charming shapes.

Two lovely celluloid purse frames; the top displays a mottled design bearing an over clasp type closure; below, a black fleur de lis theme with a plunger top. 5½. The Curiosity Shop. $500.00 – 650.00 each.

Lily of the valley toned floral frame with floral brocade pouch. 3½ x 8½. Author's collection, photograph by Irene Clarke. $700.00 – 900.00.

Marbled gray frame with pierced design and silk crocheted pouch. A linked celluloid carry chain with interwoven plaited cord provides for extra durability. 7 x 8. The Curiosity Shop, photograph by Irene Clarke. $500.00 – 650.00.

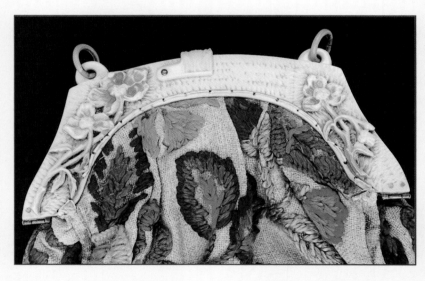

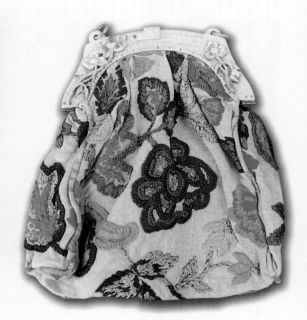

A basketweave designed floral frame heralding a flip top closure along with a hand-embroidered purse body and green silk lining. 6¼ x 9. Author's collection, photograph by Irene Clarke. $700.00 – 900.00.

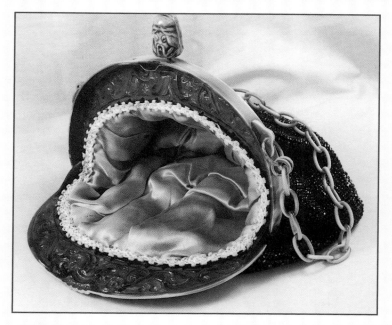

A ram's head celluloid framed purse, shown open, reveals a plush, silk lined interior complete with fancy braid trim. Bronze and black glass beaded bag body. 6¼ x 9. Author's collection, photograph by Irene Clarke. $800.00 – 1,000.00.

Ram's head purse frame, toned in color with high relief. A Mongolian face decorates the plunger top.

The center of this contrasting color celluloid purse frame emulates ivory, while the mottled brown mimics tortoise shell. A striking and colorful needlework purse body adds interest. This clearly demonstrates how pigments and dyes can change the appearance of the celluloid. Without them, celluloid would resemble gelatin or transparent horn in its original state. 9 x 9. The Curiosity Shop, photograph by Irene Clarke. $350.00 – 550.00.

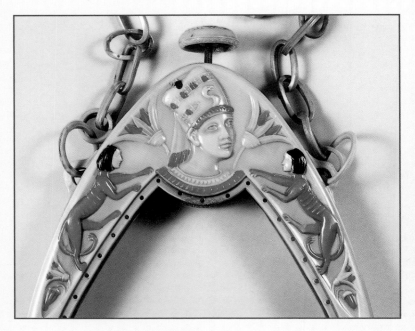

Sacred Egyptian cats with human heads, a Pharaoh, and lotus flowers decorate this colored celluloid frame. 4½. Author's collection, photograph by Irene Clarke. Rare.

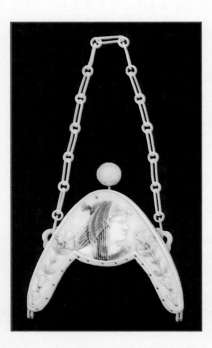

A Pharaoh, tinted in color, and Egyptian lotus decorate this ivory celluloid frame while a ball top plunger provides access. 4½. The Curiosity Shop. $450.00 – 650.00.

Sensational Sphinx motif carved and colored celluloid frame atop a stylized Egyptian motif glass beaded pouch. 4½ x 7. From the collection of Diane Goldfarb. Rare.

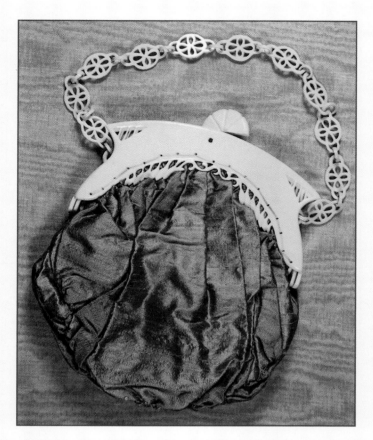

Fancy ivory finished frame with pierced corners and a unique celluloid drop design. A choice plunger top knob and intricate linked carry chain finish the look. Sea green silk pouch, cream satin lining. 5¾. The Curiosity Shop, photograph by Irene Clarke. $650.00 – 850.00.

A pair of plunger top celluloid frames. One has a raised cameo décor, the other a simple faux tortoiseshell. 5¾. The Curiosity Shop, photograph by Irene Clarke. $200.00 – 300.00 each.

Plush brown velvet bottom with domed Japanese umbrella frame top. 4½ x 7. The Curiosity Shop. Rare.

Pressed celluloid purse with leather carry cord. 4" dia. The Curiosity Shop. $300.00 – 450.00.

A purse frame made to imitate the look of ivory through the use of celluloid. Genuine ivory was scarce and more expensive to use. The use of cut iridescent glass bugle beads and pink silk gives the illusion of an overall pink appearance to the body of the bag. Looped fringe in varying length and colors. 3¼ x 7. The Curiosity Shop, photograph by Irene Clarke. $250.00 – 350.00.

Decorative domed floral celluloid purse top, plush velvet pouch. 4½ x 6. From the collection of Diane Goldfarb. $700.00 – 900.00.

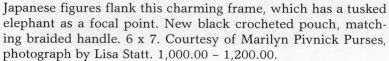

Japanese figures flank this charming frame, which has a tusked elephant as a focal point. New black crocheted pouch, matching braided handle. 6 x 7. Courtesy of Marilyn Pivnick Purses, photograph by Lisa Statt. 1,000.00 – 1,200.00.

Doves with deeply carved feathers decorate a well executed frame. Notice the embellished overclasp that is in keeping with the general design. Crocheted glass beaded body in a red and black checkerboard pattern. 5½ x 10. The Curiosity Shop. $900.00 – 1,100.00.

Sphinxes, Pharaohs, lotus, and other Egyptian symbols decorate these three celluloid purse frames. 5½ to 6½. The Curiosity Shop. $300.00 – 500.00 each.

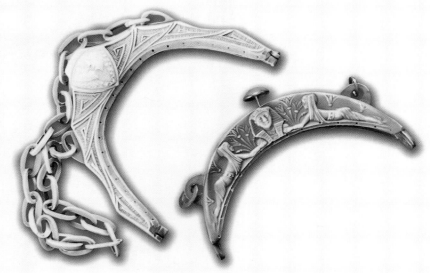

Facing Pharaohs and Egyptian handmaidens decorate an ivory colored celluloid plunger top frame. 5½. The Curiosity Shop. $350.00 – 550.00.

A pair of elephants standing on overclasps is portrayed in ivory colored celluloid purse frames. An elephant with a lifted trunk is believed to promote good luck. 3 & 5½. The Curiosity Shop, photograph by Irene Clarke. $200.00 – 400.00.

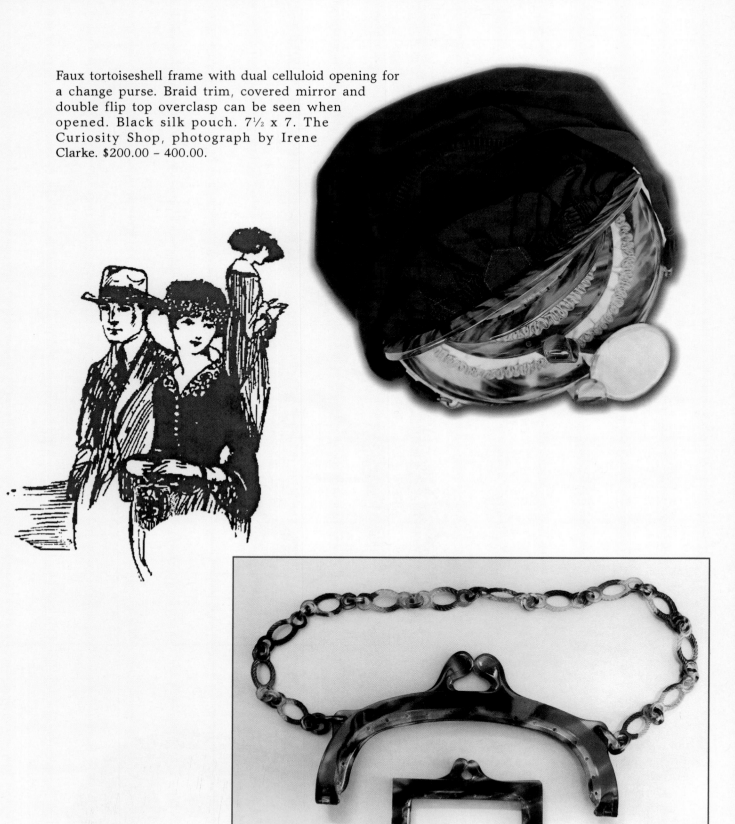

Faux tortoiseshell frame with dual celluloid opening for a change purse. Braid trim, covered mirror and double flip top overclasp can be seen when opened. Black silk pouch. 7½ x 7. The Curiosity Shop, photograph by Irene Clarke. $200.00 – 400.00.

A pair of tortoiseshell colored celluloid frames. 3 & 5½. The Curiosity Shop, photograph by Irene Clarke. $150.00 – 250.00.

Oriental toned ivory motif with Buddha and elephants. A plunger top provides access when depressed. 6". The Curiosity Shop, photograph by Irene Clarke. $200.00 – 400.00.

An ivory colored cameo swivels to provide access to the interior of this purse frame. This type of handle has a rigid finger ring which may also be used to attach a carry cord. 5¼. The Curiosity Shop, photograph by Irene Clarke. $295.00 – 395.00.

A vintage elephant overclasp tops a mottled celluloid frame. New crocheted bag. 6 x 6. Courtesy of Marilyn Pivnick Purses, photograph by Lisa Statt. $475.00 – 675.00.

Three different celluloid purse frames; one with an Oriental motif and plunger top; another with a lively peach color containing an overclasp closure; the last has a black and white checkerboard pattern with a plunger top. 5½. The Curiosity Shop. $375.00 – 675.00 each.

Imitation (celluloid) tortoiseshell frame with paisley pouch and matching carry handle. 8½. The Curiosity Shop, photograph by Irene Clarke. $500.00 – 700.00.

Most celluloid purse frames were of a simple arched variety with a single color.

Pretty floral celluloid frame with rigid handle. Seldom does the celluloid frame come complete with a matching pendant drop. Newer circular crocheted purse body. 6 x 7. Courtesy of Marilyn Pivnick Purses, photograph by Lisa Statt. $800.00 – 1,000.00.

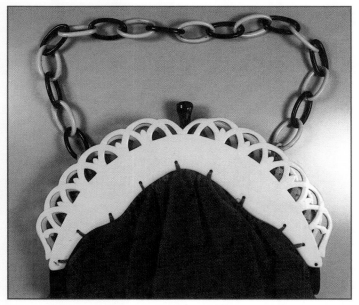

Ivory colored interestingly shaped frame with an alternating colored carry chain. Brown velvet pouch. 6½ x 7. The Curiosity Shop, photograph by Irene Clarke. $395.00 – 595.00.

Beaded change purse on ivory colored frame. 2¾ x 3½. The Curiosity Shop, photograph by Irene Clarke. $155.00 – 225.00.

Worked on fine netted gauze, this medium glass beaded bag shows the solar disc, a winged scarab and lotus blossoms. The celluloid frame has stamped Egyptian figures, including a Sphinx. 8 x 10. The Curiosity Shop. $700.00 – 900.00.

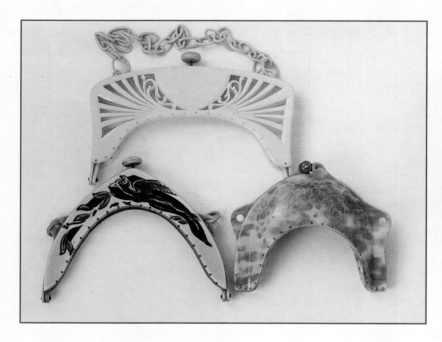

Celluloid frames vary in size, shape, and style. Shown is a carved figural bird in color with ivory openwork design, and a mottled dome shape frame. 4½ – 6. The Curiosity Shop. $400.00 – 600.00 each.

Abstract floral glass beaded purse with simple faux tortoiseshell frame, plunger top, beaded carry handle. 6½ x 8. The Curiosity Shop, photograph by Irene Clarke. $350.00 – 550.00.

Semicircle celluloid tortoiseshell frame with overclasp. Blue glass beading is finished with a large knotted tassel. 5½. The Curiosity Shop, photograph by Irene Clarke. $400.00 – 600.00.

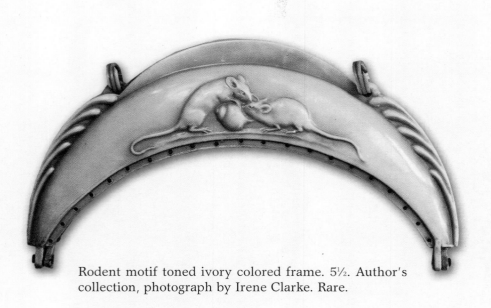

Rodent motif toned ivory colored frame. 5½. Author's
collection, photograph by Irene Clarke. Rare.

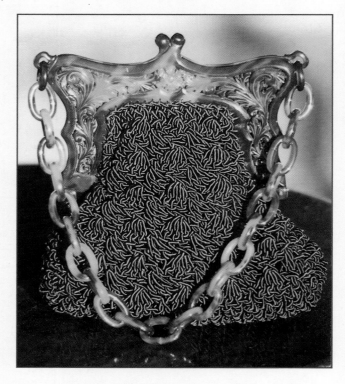

Ornate faux tortoiseshell frame, sturdy linked cellu-
loid carry chain, newer crocheted pouch. 6 x 6.
Courtesy of Marilyn Pivnick Purses, photograph by
Lisa Statt. $600.00 – 800.00.

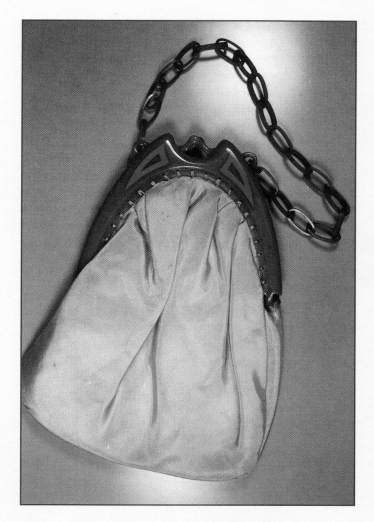

Art deco designed early plastic green frame decorated with red painting. Silk pouch. 4½. The Curiosity Shop, photograph by Irene Clarke. $275.00 – 475.00.

Egyptian views in toned ivory celluloid. 7". The Curiosity Shop, photograph by Irene Clarke. $695.00 – 895.00.

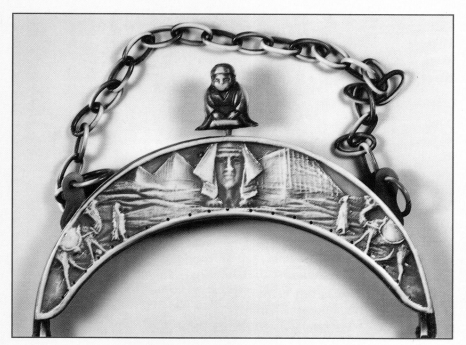

Butterscotch colored celluloid plunger top frame in a simple design pictured with an intricate black and white elephant motif. The depressor from the plunger top is missing. 5½ – 6. The Curiosity Shop, photograph by Irene Clarke. $200.00 – 300.00 if perfect.

A heavily carved long tailed snarling dragon motif celluloid frame with a garish floral beaded purse body. 5½ x 10. The Curiosity Shop. $800.00 – 1,000.00.

Hidden double depth pierced design frame, blue silk pouch with piping and pink silk lining. 7 x 8. The Curiosity Shop, photograph by Irene Clarke. $495.00 – 695.00.

A variety of celluloid purse frames in various colors, shapes, and designs. 5½ – 6. The Curiosity Shop. $295.00 – 395.00 each.

Marked "Made in France," an arched tortoiseshell colored frame enhances a dusty rose floral beaded pouch with a beaded carry cord. 6 x 8. The Curiosity Shop, photograph by Irene Clarke. $375.00 – 575.00.

Toned ivory celluloid open work frame with linked carry chain. 5½. The Curiosity Shop, photograph by Irene Clarke. $350.00 – 550.00.

Flappers model a variety of purses.

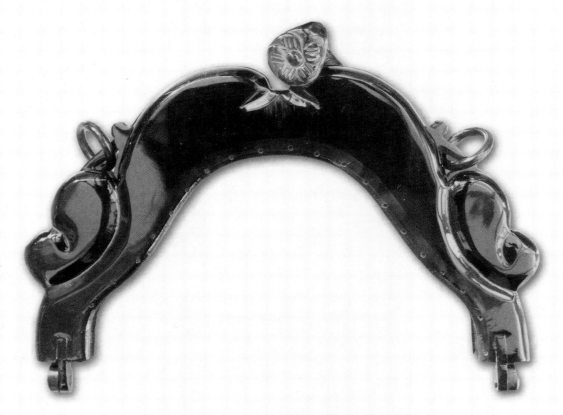

Chunky early plastic frame with a carved floral closure in dark tortoise shell. 6". The Curiosity Shop, photograph by Irene Clarke. $400.00 – 600.00.

A sleek striped design adorns this celluloid frame and pretty glass beaded pouch in a floral design. 6 x 9½. The Curiosity Shop. $550.00 – 750.00.

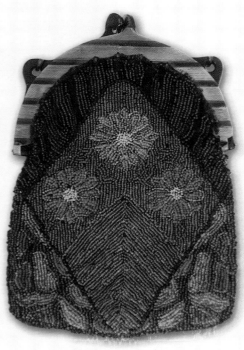

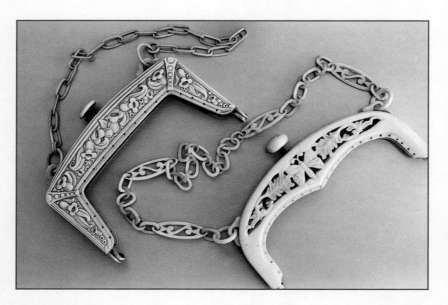

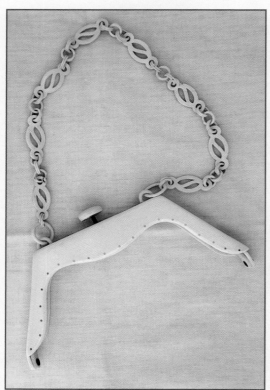

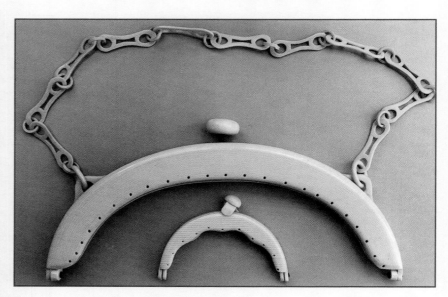

Celluloid and early purse frames
were manufactured in a variety of
shapes, sizes, and colors.

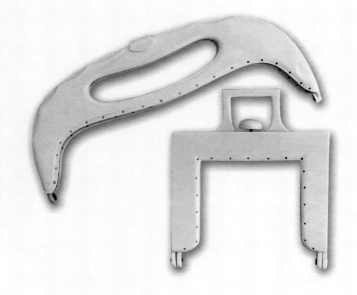

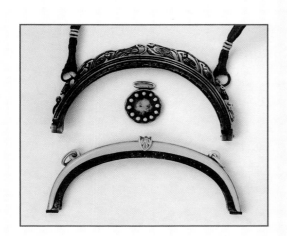

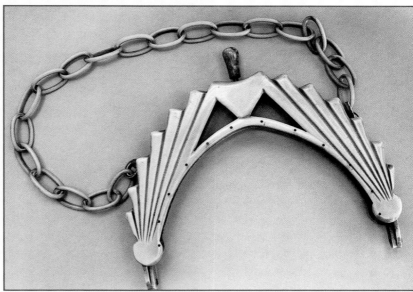

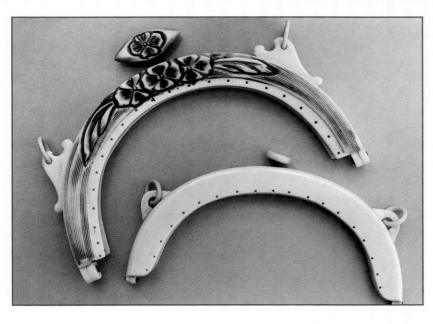

Bibliography

A Distinctive Group of Beaded Bags. Dritz-Traum Company, 1925.

Ball, Joanne Dubbs. *Costume Jewelers, The Golden Age of Design*. Atglen, Pennsylvania: Schiffer Publishing, Ltd., 1990.

Bell, Jeanenne. *Answers to Questions about Old Jewelry*. Florence, Alabama: Books Americana, 1992.

Canaday, John. *Mainstreams of Modern Art, The New York Times*. New York, New York: Holt, Rinehart and Winston, 1959.

Chilvers, Ian; Dennis Farr and Harold Osborne. *The Oxford Dictionary of Art*. Oxford University Press, 1994.

End of World Art. New York, Toronto, London: McGraw Hill, 1965.

Gallup, Alison; Gerhard Gruitrooy and Elizabeth M. Weisberg. *Great Paintings of the Western World*. Hugh Lauter Levin Associates, Inc., 1998.

Gowing, Sir Lawrence. *A History of Art*. 1995.

Great Artists of the Western World, French Rococo. London; New York: Marshall Carendish Ltd., 1987.

Great Artists of the Western World. London; New York: Marshall Carendish Ltd., 1987.

Great Artists of the Western World, The French Classical Tradition. London; New York: Marshall Carendish Ltd., 1987.

Great Artists of the Western World, The High Renaissance. London; New York: Marshall Carendish Ltd., 1987.

Gregori, Mina. *Paintings in the Uffizi and Pitti Galleries*. Boston, Massachusetts: A Bulfinch Press Book, 1994.

Haertig, Evelyn. *More Beautiful Purses*. Carmel, Californua: Gallery Graphics Press, 1990.

Jeweler's Circular, The, 1929.

Levey, Michael. *A Concise History of Painting*. Thames and Hudson Inc., 1994.

Miller, Harrice Simons. *Costume Jewelry Identification*. Morrow, William & Company, 1993.

Oggins, Robin S. *Castles and Fortresses*. Freidman/Fairfax Publishers. 1995, 2000.

Ottendorf-Simrock, Dr Walther. *Castles on the Rhein*, 2nd Edition. Wilelm Stollfus Verlag Bonn.

Poe, Edgar Allen. *The Poetical Works of Edgar Allen Poe*. New York: Weathervane Books, 1978.

Priscilla Bead Work Book. Boston, Massachusetts: The Priscilla Publishing Co., 1912.

Schwartz, Lynell K. *Vintage Purses at Their Best*. Atglen, Pennsylvania: Schiffer Publishing, Ltd., 1995.

------. *Vintage Compacts and Beauty Accessories*. Atglen, Pennsylvania: Schiffer Publishing, Ltd., 1997.

Zahn, Peter von. *Farbiges Deutschland*. Germany, 1986.

Websites

bau2.uibk.ac.at/sg/poe/works/poetry/raven.html

www.artchive.com/artchive/R/raphael.html Raphael (Raffaello Sanzio)

www.WhitingDavis.thomasregister.com.

www.ucpress.edu/books/pages/8377.html The Portraits of Madame de Pompadour by Elise Goodman, The Discovery Series.

Exhibits

Treasures of Tutankhamun, The Metropolitan Museum of Art, 1976.

Lynell Schwartz is the author of *Vintage Purses at Their Best* and *Vintage Compacts and Beauty Accessories*. Owner of The Curiosity Shop in Cheshire, Connecticut, for more than a decade, her articles and antiques have appeared in many national magazines and newspapers, including *Antiques and the Arts Weekly* and *The Maine Antiques Digest*. She has been a consultant for Reuters News and has authored several children's stories including *The Winged Horse*.

Ms. Schwartz is a member of the Connecticut Association of Dealers in Antiques, Inc. She continues to exhibit at leading shows and actively buys and sells estates, specializing in ladies' accessories, costume and antique jewelry, compacts, purses, and purse frames. She has been featured on The Discovery Channel's *Home Matters* with Susan Powell and *Calling All Collectors*. She is nationally recognized as an authority on ladies' vintage accessories and is publisher of the purse collector's newsletter. Any correspondence with SASE can be directed to: The Curiosity Shop, P.O. Box 964, Cheshire, CT 06410.

GLASSWARE & POTTERY

4929	**American Art Pottery**, 1880 – 1950, Sigafoose	$24.95
5907	Collector's Encyclopedia of **Depression Glass**, 15th Ed., Florence	$19.95
5748	Collector's Encyclopedia of **Fiesta**, 9th Ed., Huxford	$24.95
5609	Collector's Encyclopedia of **Limoges Porcelain**, 3rd Ed., Gaston	$29.95
1358	Collector's Encyclopedia of **McCoy Pottery**, Huxford	$19.95
5677	Collector's Encyclopedia of **Niloak**, 2nd Edition, Gifford	$29.95
5678	Collector's Encyclopedia of **Nippon Porcelain**, 6th Series, Van Patten	$29.95
5618	Collector's Encyclopedia of **Rosemeade Pottery**, Dommel	$24.95
5842	Collector's Encyclopedia of **Roseville Pottery**, Vol. 2, Huxford/Nickel	$24.95
5921	Collector's Encyclopedia of **Stangl Artware**, Lamps, and Birds, Runge	$29.95
5680	Collector's Guide to **Feather Edge Ware**, McAllister	$19.95
6124	Collector's Guide to **Made In Japan Ceramics**, Book IV, White	$24.95
1523	Colors in **Cambridge Glass**, National Cambridge Society	$19.95
4714	**Czechoslovakian Glass** and Collectibles, Book II, Barta	$16.95
5528	Early American **Pattern Glass**, Metz	$17.95
5257	**Fenton Art Glass** Patterns, 1939 – 1980, Whitmyer	$29.95
5261	**Fostoria Tableware**, 1924 – 1943, Long/Seate	$24.95
5899	**Glass & Ceramic Baskets**, White	$19.95
6127	The **Glass Candlestick** Book, Vol. 1, Akro Agate to Fenton, Felt/Stoer	$24.95
5840	**Heisey Glass**, 1896 – 1957, Bredehoft	$24.95
6135	**North Carolina Art Pottery**, 1900 – 1960, James/Leftwich	$24.95
5691	**Post86 Fiesta**, Identification & Value Guide, Racheter	$19.95
6037	**Rookwood Pottery**, Nicholson/Thomas	$24.95
5924	**Zanesville Stoneware** Company, Rans, Ralston & Russell	$24.95

DOLLS, FIGURES & TEDDY BEARS

2079	**Barbie** Doll Fashion, Volume I, Eames	$24.95
3957	**Barbie** Exclusives, Rana	$18.95
6022	The **Barbie** Doll Years, 5th Edition, Olds	$19.95
3810	**Chatty Cathy** Dolls, Lewis	$15.95
4559	Collectible **Action Figures**, 2nd Ed., Manos	$17.95
6134	Ency. of Bisque **Nancy Ann** Storybook Dolls, 1936 – 1947, Pardee/Robertson	$29.95
4863	Collector's Encyclopedia of **Vogue Dolls**, Stover/Izen	$29.95
5904	Collector's Guide to **Celebrity Dolls**, Spurgeon	$24.95
1799	**Effanbee Dolls**, Smith	$19.95
5611	**Madame Alexander** Store Exclusives & Limited Editions, Crowsey	$24.95
5689	**Nippon Dolls** & Playthings, Van Patten/Lau	$29.95
5253	Story of **Barbie**, 2nd Ed., Westenhouser	$24.95
1513	**Teddy Bears** & **Steiff** Animals, Mandel	$9.95
1808	Wonder of **Barbie**, Manos	$9.95
1430	World of **Barbie** Dolls, Manos	$9.95
4880	World of **Raggedy Ann** Collectibles, Avery	$24.95

JEWELRY, HATPINS & PURSES

1748	**Antique Purses**, Revised Second Ed., Holiner	$19.95
4850	Collectible **Costume Jewelry**, Simonds	$24.95
5675	Collectible **Silver Jewelry**, Rezazadeh	$24.95
3722	Collector's Ency. of **Compacts**, Carryalls & Face Powder Boxes, Mueller	$24.95
4940	**Costume Jewelry**, A Practical Handbook & Value Guide, Rezazadeh	$24.95
5812	Fifty Years of Collectible Fashion **Jewelry**, 1925-1975, Baker	$24.95
1424	**Hatpins** & Hatpin Holders, Baker	$9.95
5695	**Ladies' Vintage Accessories**, Bruton	$24.95
1181	100 Years of Collectible **Jewelry**, 1850 – 1950, Baker	$9.95
6232	**Plastic Jewelry** of the 20th Century, Baker	$24.95
6039	Signed Beauties of **Costume Jewelry**, Brown	$24.95
4850	Unsigned Beauties of **Costume Jewelry**, Brown	$24.95
5696	Vintage & Vogue Ladies' **Compacts**, 2nd Edition, Gerson	$29.95
5923	**Vintage Jewelry** for Investment & Casual Wear, Edeen	$24.95

FURNITURE

3716	American **Oak** Furniture, Book II, McNerney	$12.95
1118	Antique **Oak** Furniture, Hill	$7.95
3720	Collector's Encyclopedia of **American** Furniture, Vol. III, Swedberg	$24.95
5359	Early **American** Furniture, Obbard	$12.95
3906	**Heywood-Wakefield** Modern Furniture, Rouland	$18.95
1885	**Victorian** Furniture, Our American Heritage, McNerney	$9.95
3829	**Victorian** Furniture, Our American Heritage, Book II, McNerney	$9.95

INDIANS, GUNS, KNIVES, TOOLS, PRIMITIVES

1868	**Antique Tools**, Our American Heritage, McNerney	$9.95
1426	**Arrowheads** & Projectile Points, Hothem	$7.95
6021	**Arrowheads** of the Central Great Plains, Fox	$19.95
5616	Big Book of **Pocket Knives**, Stewart	$19.95
5685	**Indian Artifacts** of the Midwest, Book IV, Hothem	$19.95
5826	**Indian Axes** & Related Stone Artifacts, 2nd Edition, Hothem	$19.95
6130	**Indian Trade Relics**, Hothem	$29.95
6132	Modern **Guns**, Identification & Values, 14th Ed., Quertermous	$14.95
2164	**Primitives**, Our American Heritage, McNerney	$9.95
1759	**Primitives**, Our American Heritage, Series II, McNerney	$14.95
6031	Standard **Knife** Collector's Guide, 4th Ed., Ritchie & Stewart	$14.95

PAPER COLLECTIBLES & BOOKS

4633	**Big Little Books**, A Collector's Reference & Value Guide, Jacobs	$18.95
5902	**Boys' & Girls' Book** Series, Jones	$19.95
4710	Collector's Guide to **Children's Books**, Vol. I, Jones	$18.95
5153	Collector's Guide to **Children's Books**, Vol. II, Jones	$19.95
1441	Collector's Guide to **Post Cards**, Wood	$9.95
2081	Guide to Collecting **Cookbooks**, Allen	$14.95
2080	Price Guide to **Cookbooks** & Recipe Leaflets, Dickinson	$9.95
4733	**Whitman Juvenile Books**, Brown	$17.95

TOYS & MARBLES

2333	Antique & Collectible **Marbles**, 3rd Ed., Grist	$9.95
5681	Collector's Guide to **Lunchboxes**, White	$19.95
4566	Collector's Guide to **Tootsietoys**, 2nd Ed, Richter	$19.95
4945	**G-Men and FBI Toys**, Whitworth	$18.95
5593	Grist's Big Book of **Marbles**, 2nd Ed.	$24.95
3970	Grist's Machine-Made & Contemporary **Marbles**, 2nd Ed.	$9.95
6128	**Hot Wheels**, The Ultimate Redline Guide, 1968 – 1977, Clark/Wicker	$24.95
5267	**Matchbox Toys**, 3rd Ed., 1947 to 1998, Johnson	$19.95
5830	**McDonald's** Collectibles, Henriques/DuVall	$24.95
5673	Modern **Candy Containers** & Novelties, Brush/Miller	$19.95
1540	Modern **Toys** 1930–1980, Baker	$19.95
5920	Schroeder's **Collectible Toys**, Antique to Modern Price Guide, 8th Ed	$17.95
6140	**Teddy Bear** Treasury, Vol. II, Yenke	$24.95
5908	**Toy Car** Collector's Guide, Johnson	$19.95

OTHER COLLECTIBLES

5898	Antique & Contemporary **Advertising Memorabilia**, Summers	$24.95
5814	Antique **Brass & Copper** Collectibles, Gaston	$24.95
1880	Antique **Iron**, McNerney	$9.95
3872	Antique **Tins**, Dodge	$24.95
3718	Antiquing and Collecting on the **Internet**, Parry	$12.95
1128	**Bottle** Pricing Guide, 3rd Ed., Cleveland	$7.95
3718	Collectible **Aluminum**, Grist	$16.95
5676	Collectible **Souvenir Spoons**, Book II, Bednersh	$29.95
5666	Collector's Encyclopedia of **Granite Ware**, Book II, Greguire	$29.95
4857	Collector's Guide to **Art Deco**, 2nd Ed., Gaston	$17.95
5906	Collector's Guide to **Creek Chub Lures** & Collectibles, 2nd Ed., Smith	$29.95
3966	Collector's Guide to **Inkwells**, Identification & Values, Badders	$18.95
3881	Collector's Guide to **Novelty Radios**, Bunis/Breed	$18.95
4864	Collector's Guide to **Wallace Nutting Pictures**, Ivankovich	$18.95
5929	Commercial **Fish Decoys**, Baron	$29.95
5683	**Fishing Lure Collectibles**, Vol. 1, Murphy/Edmisten	$29.95
6141	**Fishing Lure Collectibles**, Vol. 2, Murphy	$29.95
5911	**Flea Market Trader**, 13th Ed., Huxford	$9.95
5262	**Fountain Pens**, Erano	$24.95
6227	**Garage Sale** & Flea Market Annual, 11th Edition, Huxford	$19.95
3819	**General Store** Collectibles, Wilson	$24.95
2216	**Kitchen Antiques**, 1790–1940, McNerney	$14.95
5686	**Lighting Fixtures** of the Depression Era, Book I, Thomas	$24.95
5603	19th Century **Fishing Lures**, Carter	$29.95
5835	**Racing** Collectibles	$19.95
2026	**Railroad** Collectibles, 4th Ed., Baker	$14.95
5619	**Roy Rogers and Dale Evans** Toys & Memorabilia, Coyle	$24.95
1632	**Salt & Pepper Shakers**, Guarnaccia	$9.95
5091	**Salt & Pepper Shakers** II, Guarnaccia	$18.95
3443	**Salt & Pepper Shakers** IV, Guarnaccia	$18.95
6137	**Schroeder's Antiques** Price Guide, 21st Edition 2003	$14.95
5007	**Silverplated Flatware**, Revised 4th Edition, Hagan	$18.95
6239	**Star Wars** Super Collector's Wish Book, 2nd Ed., Carlton	$29.95
3977	Value Guide to **Gas Station Memorabilia**, Summers	$24.95
4877	Vintage **Bar Ware**, Visakay	$24.95
5925	The Vintage Era of **Golf Club** Collectibles, John	$29.95
4935	The W.F. Cody **Buffalo Bill** Collector's Guide with Values, Wojtowicz	$24.95

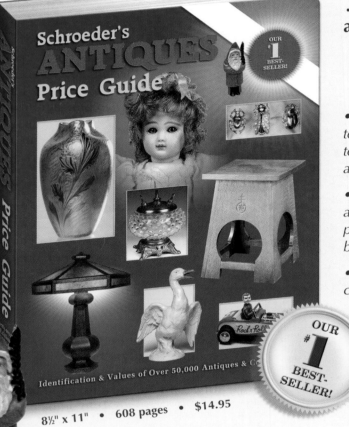

PLAINVILLE STOCK COMPANY.
MANUFACTURING JEWELERS.

PLAINVILLE STOCK COMPANY